We are here to know ourselves

a journey to discover you

Gary Bate

Blue Light Publishing
www.bluelightpublishing.com

We are here to know ourselves

Copyright Gary Bate 2000 - 2009.

All Rights Reserved.

No part of this book may be reproduced in any form
by photocopying or by any electronic or mechanical means,
including information storage or retrieval systems,
without permission in writing from both the copyright
owner and the publisher of this book.

All the direct Ramtha quotes in this publication are used
with permission from JZK Publishing, a division of JZK, Inc.

No part of these direct quotes, including any artwork and images
published by JZK, Inc., may be reproduced or transmitted in any
form or by any means, electronic or mechanical, including
photocopying, recording, or by any information storage and retrieval
systems, without the written permission of JZK Publishing,
a division of JZK, Inc. All rights reserved.

ISBN 0-9545280-7-7

Second Edition Published January 2009.

CONTENTS

Foreword 5

Part 1 - Ride with the Wind

Introduction 7
The journey begins 8
Football crowds in Church 11
My God is not in any Religion 13
Separated from the Whole 15
Karma is only a limited Truth 16
An Aussie shocker 18
Out-of-Body experiences 20
A Light floating on a sea of Darkness 24
All aboard with Ron 27
Everything is spiritual in its own way 30
My weird friend Euwen 34
Butt heads with the Ram 36
The journey of your Soul 41
Cinema 2000 43
The Children of Blue Light 52
What is Reality? 57

Part 2 - The Blue Window

Introduction 61
Mind control 63
Free will 67
Truth 69
Perfection 71
Identity trap 72
Responsibility 76
Unconditional love 80
God and Science 81
Body energy centres 84
Evolution 94
Sex and relationships 98
Attitude is everything 109
The Box 112

Continued...

Come dive with me 114
Human potential 116
Demons and Judgement 118
Fairness and Equality 124
Soul destiny or merry-go-round? 127
The Blue Window 129

Part 3 - Becoming a Master

Introduction 134
Becoming a Master 136
The Secret of Happiness 141
Cultivate your mind 142
A new life 148
And finally 151

FOREWORD

I imagine it to be common knowledge that a masterful, enlightened being, would attribute their personal growth to 'knowing thyself' or 'conquering thyself'. Hence the title of my work – We are here to know ourselves.

This is a personal journey of self-discovery, to share wisdom, the pearls one needs in order to 'let go'. Indeed, there is no letting go without the appropriate wisdom, which emphasises the importance of this to you.

Letting go of what, you may be asking? Of all that is illusionary of course! The World teaches us to try and be successful by adding more 'pieces of image'; yet the master knows that bliss is reached by burning those images from self.

We are here to know ourselves is the book that will put you on the true Spiritual path and its sequel, The Question is, will radically accelerate you.

Everyone has one or more psychological weaknesses and often we don't see it in ourselves because we're too busy being it. Even when someone points it out, it can often take a long time before we fully accept it. Then it can take an even longer time before we completely overcome it.

So what is the effect of 'owning' a weakness and what does it effectively mean? The effect is, you remove that bias from your psyche and you see more clearly (you have removed the lens you were previously viewing through). It means you have taken a step up in your evolution.

Owning all of your weaknesses is climbing all the way to the top of the consciousness pyramid. Can you ever imagine doing that? What would that look like? Imagine if you reached a point where you treated all men and all women exactly the same, with unconditional love, that is what it looks like.

Everything is about relative importance. What is important to one person is not as important to another person and vice versa. Changing the relative importance in your life is owning your life.

The problem we all seem to have is not recognising when an experience is over. It's not offering us anything new but we hang on in there because we are simply addicted to it and or we haven't got the wisdom from it.

The only motive for writing this book is to provoke thought in you, to get you to question and to help you on your journey in life. In parts, you may find the content to be somewhat controversial. It is a combination of my truth from my experiences and my interpretation of what I have learned from others who have influenced me.

This is not a book that is going to necessarily make you a material success; nor is it a book that will necessarily make your life any better or more comfortable in the short-term. *There are many different ways of looking at many different things in your life.* This is primarily a book for people who want to advance themselves spiritually, who want to evolve themselves beyond their human conditioning and who eventually want to accept they can live in a loving, joyous state of mind.

I do hope you will enjoy reading my book and that it gives you many hours of mind-expanding contemplation. If, however, you go into denial or you doubt or you disagree with any part of my work; then please just keep an open mind and the truth will be revealed to you through the course of your own experiences.

If you have any questions or you want to share anything with me, then please do not hesitate to contact me through my website, which is:

www.whatstress.com

Part 1

Ride with the Wind

INTRODUCTION

This first part is a shortened biography, my journey of self-discovery that has led me to my present-day understanding. I felt it was necessary for you to get an insight into my life in order to help you to understand how I have come to certain realisations and why I have decided to share this life-changing wisdom with you.

Hello and welcome to my book! For many years I have had the inspiration to put pen to paper but until now I had doubted my knowledge and abilities with thoughts such as, 'what could I possibly know that would be of interest to others, especially ordinary folk, like myself?' Also, what were my motives for wanting to write to mankind? You see, often the motives we portray to others aren't our real motives. So I had to do a lot of soul-searching to see if there were any ulterior motives. This was very important to me because I only wanted to write to you if it was for unselfish reasons. I am pleased to say that my only motive is to share information and to provoke thought in you.

All of my life I have been trying to get answers to the bare mysteries of this life in my quest for a greater truth. I have been an extremely self-centred person, which for the most part, has served me well in the 'dog-eat-dog' society that we live in. Now that I have realised my answers, I have flipped over the coin and am now sharing my experiences with you.

In this book I will focus upon humanity's transition from an existing social consciousness to a state of super consciousness, which also means my own personal transformation. I will take a look at how we live life today and what shapes our created realities and our individual destinies. I will also show how we can move beyond our illusions and the effects of our mind-controlled society. The result is the becoming of a super-conscious, free-thinking society of authentically, powerful individuals.

I reckon it will take at least five years to shift the collective consciousness of humanity sufficiently enough to make a significant enough difference to our environment and to our planetary living conditions. And this will not be without pain, suffering and death.

I do hope you will join with me in this evolutionary process. Together we can reach a greater understanding and make a big difference to the way we live life.

Ride with the Wind

THE JOURNEY BEGINS

From about age five I would look out of my bedroom window at night and gaze into the night sky at the wonderment of infinity, the stars and those seemingly faraway places, the pale moon with her soft light and the majestic sun. In summertime, I would watch the sun disappear over the horizon. It always seemed so close to me that I felt I could reach out and touch it. Have you ever wondered why as children we have these feelings? Is there some innate wisdom that we are closer to as children that we all forget about when we become adults?

Like all of you, my childhood was subjected to a certain amount of abuse, both physical and mental, but it was still magical. I am not wishing to imply here that my parents physically abused me, for this is not the case. I did, however, lose my innocence in an incident involving an older boy at a young age, the significance of that happening, I will reveal later. The mental abuse I refer to is what most children suffer from as a result of the conditioning by society of their parents.

Can you remember some of the magic from your childhood? Or was it mainly suffering? Why do some of us suffer more or less than others? And why is it as children we find it easier to forgive and to love? Could it be that we are closer to that which we really are as children?

As a child I was fearless, I had no worries. I was daring, adventurous, cunning, mischievous, full of life and one with life. Like most kids I loved the outdoors. I loved nature, the animals, the birds, the trees, the open fields, the blue sky and so on. My friends and I would go out and play and get lost in ourselves; time would just collapse. Does this not tell us something? Have you had similar childhood experiences?

By the time we hit junior school we have already become conditioned by society. You see, as children, we do not think like adults; we do not judge thought. It is pure thought, unjudged. It feeds our imaginations, draws pictures in our minds, and allows us to be creative and to have all potentials. And it allows us to have friends in the unseen dimensions of life.

Only recently I listened to a conversation in a friend's hairdressing salon. A young girl was having her haircut and the stylist asked her what she would like to be when she grew up. The young girl proceeded to tell the stylist of her dream of owning a farm and went on to describe the animals on her farm.

The young girl's father retorted, 'stop carrying on, you'll never have a farm, take no notice of her!'

Ride with the Wind

The stylist and I were obviously shocked by this response. Isn't this kind of mental abuse all too common? Can you think of any examples? For God's sake, it's our choice if we choose to hold ourselves back in life because of the limiting way in which we think, but let's stop abusing our kids by annihilating their dreams - the very power they have to create in their lives.

Never tell your children, "It's only your imagination". Imagination is reality. Let me give you an example. A father is teaching his young daughter to ride her first bike without stabilisers. The daughter is happy riding the bike with the knowledge that her father is balancing her by holding the rear of the saddle. What she doesn't know is that her father has let go of the saddle and still walks alongside her. What is the reality? The daughter's reality is her imagination - she is riding her bike with the help of her father. The father's reality is his thoughts based upon his observation - that his daughter is riding her bike unaided. Which one is correct? Both are! Most of society believes that reality is what is agreed upon by the majority in any given situation and people argue amongst themselves accordingly, whereas I am suggesting that everyone's reality is different and is the result of their thinking only.

As children we have no concept of good and bad, right and wrong and other polarities, and therefore we do not suffer as adults do from shame and guilt. However, as children, our minds are responsive to the environment that we live in, which normally consists of adults who have previously been conditioned into limited thinking by their parents and society in general. From our parents, grandparents, school teachers, religious men, television and other dominant influences we learn about good and bad, right and wrong, being a sinner, hero worship, God being superior to us and outside of us, violence, anger, hatred, resentment, possessiveness, jealously, power over others, victim mode, feeling betrayed, conditional love and all the other niceties that we find in social consciousness. We are moved from being pure Godlike beings with open-minds to impure image-conscious beings with closed minds.

During adolescence I remember lying awake at nights wondering, what is the purpose of this life? Is there a God and if so who made God? When was the beginning and how did it come about? Does life end when we go to the grave? What if there never was a beginning and never is an end? What is this hideous creature called the Devil? And if the Devil does exist and it is so evil why doesn't this all-powerful God of ours just annihilate it? What am I? And where do I fit in with this unknown God? Why doesn't anyone have any answers for me or at least show some interest? The only answer that came through to me at that time was, **you are the sum total of your experiences**, which I can totally relate to even today. Could that be the purpose of our lives - to have experiences that teach us about ourselves and about life in general?

Ride with the Wind

From an early age I would think about the sun and its relationship to us and to all life. What would happen if the sun never rose again in the morning? And worse still, what would happen if you looked into the sky at night and there was no moon or stars either? Life as we know it would simply not exist. So are we really separate from the planets and other life? And if there is a God and it is the source of all life then the suns, moons, other planets and stars can only be a part of it, and a significant part too. Are we really separate from other forms of life and this unknown God that we all seem to be so confused by?

These days we take it for granted that the sun will rise every morning to light up the world and nourish the plant life, which in turn gives us the oxygen we need to breathe. We have a very tenuous relationship with our mother, Mother Nature, and yet we are abusing her! We cause massive splinters in her skin and send shock waves through the universe with nuclear testing. We use our seas as dumping grounds for radioactive and other toxic waste that is killing the sea life. We are killing great animals and mammals many of which are verging upon extinction. We poison our atmosphere with toxic gases and cut or burn down the trees in the name of 'progress' - the very trees we need to sustain our lives! When is all this stupidity going to stop?

Ride with the Wind

FOOTBALL CROWDS IN CHURCH

My teenage years were very eventful to say the least. I went to an all boys grammar school and passed ten out of eleven of my final examinations. I was simply good at retaining what has since proven to be mostly useless information. My best subject was mathematics which I have never had cause to use. My worst subject was English Language - I'll let you be the judge of my progress! I never learned anything at school that has helped to steer the course of my life. It was all insignificant knowledge coming from limited minds.

Why weren't we taught at school how to create reality using the power of our minds, like what was taught in the ancient schools of wisdom?

Our schooling system, which supposedly is to teach, actually restricts the thinking processes of our children. Through it they lose the ability to use their minds for creative purposes. We are breeding another generation of intellectuals who are spiritually (creatively) derelict. And we wonder why we are experiencing more and more problems with our kids these days!

After I left school I eventually settled into a good job working for a local firm and spent most of my free time being a typical teenager, playing soccer, partying, drinking copious amounts of alcohol and indulging in the pleasures of female company. I was fortunate in not being exposed to hard drugs, although the alcohol was hard enough! It wasn't until my early twenties that I settled into a steady relationship and this led me to go overseas to Auckland, New Zealand.

Whilst I was there, I pursued a career as an Insurance Broker and Investment Adviser. It was during this time that the financial markets between New Zealand and Australia deregulated, meaning that Australian Investment Houses could offer their products to the Kiwis. And that's exactly what they did. There came a plethora of 'off the page' advertising from Australian Unit Trust Managers, appearing in the New Zealand Herald but not in the Auckland paper, the Auckland Star, which has a smaller circulation.

It occurred to me that if I could put the same adverts in the Auckland paper with my company name on the coupon response mechanism, then there was a potential profit to be made. To cut a long story short that's exactly what I did and I made a nice profit. The most substantial investment I attracted came from a very pleasant gentleman named Stan who is a devout Christian and a member of a local church.

Stan was about forty years of age at the time, married with a young family and living in a suburb of Auckland. He was a tall and straight man, with hair thinning on top, and he wore thick-rimmed glasses. He always had a smile and he kind of

Ride with the Wind

beamed at you :) After we had concluded business he invited me to meet his family and to have dinner with them. I gladly accepted because of his friendly nature, not realising his ulterior motive at the time. When he said grace before dinner it became obvious to me that this was a man of the church, in fact, he was a real Bible-basher! Nevertheless, I was interested because I was intrigued by religion and wanted to know more; maybe it could answer some of my questions?

The following week I went with Stan to his local Baptist church and met some of his and his wife's friends; they were all dressed very smartly. I shall always remember the experience because most of the congregation had their hands raised high and were swaying just like a football crowd without the scarves! And there were some older people muttering in the corner, 'talking in tongues' so I was told. Stan and one of his 'brothers' encouraged me to go forward to the altar when the vicar said it was time for newcomers to come and denounce their sins. *This was really a commitment to the church and not to God.* I wasn't entirely comfortable with this, it just didn't feel right, but I decided to go with the flow to satisfy my curiosity, if nothing else. After church, Stan and I walked and chatted for a short while and I agreed to do a discipleship course.

Every week for the next twelve weeks I would visit Stan's home and sit with him in his caravan on his front lawn, doing assigned study. I was hoping to get some answers to my questions about the meaning of this life! However, it quickly became apparent to me that we were getting nowhere fast - neither Stan nor his Bible could answer my questions and the study was just provoking more questions in me, which Stan could not answer nor find any reference to in his Bible. I did, however, complete the course but found the experience to be most unsatisfactory and frustrating.

So what did I learn from my experience of Western religion? Not a fat lot! I learned about fanaticism and how when you become fanatical about anything you become unbalanced inwardly and this affects your outlook on life. I learned how people become so rigid when they cocoon themselves in a belief system, something they have given their power away to. This can apply equally to any group, person, place or thing that we give our power away to. I learned how mankind, through religion, has enslaved itself by giving away its power to a perceived higher authority that really only exists in the minds of men and women and that this has been a clever plan devised by the men of the Church to dethrone us from our divinity; thus increasing the power and wealth of the Church.

If we give our power away to a belief that our only route to God is through the teachings of the Church, the one and only Son who died for our sins, then we are truly enslaved creatures. We can never evolve to be that which we truly are if we succumb to this dogmatic regime.

Ride with the Wind

MY GOD IS NOT IN ANY RELIGION

So what about this chappie called God? From an early age we have it drilled into us that God is outside of us, out of our reach, an all-powerful Father figure who just sits up there somewhere on his rock, with his staff in his hand and his one and only Son at his side. He supposedly sits there watching over us to spot our mistakes so that he can make a decision whether or not to throw us into Hell and damnation with this evil creature called the Devil. Do you not think that if there were such a God he'd have something better to do? I can hear you all saying, 'well, he has got better things to do, that's why he leaves most of the day-to-day stuff to his helpers, the Pope and the other religious men'. God help us! And for goodness sake, make sure you believe in his one and only Son otherwise you'll never be saved! Don't you think it's about time we all grew up a bit?

Is God a Father or Mother figure or neither or both? What if God is a woman? That would change things a bit! And for the better too. You women readers would then get your souls back and stop believing that your salvation lay in the hands of us men. And what about if God was unisex or of neither sex? So you can come to your own conclusions I will continue by referring to God in an impersonal way, as the Mother/Father principal or simply as the Father. Where I do refer to the masculine I am inferring both genders. Woman is man with a womb.

The foundations of the world's religions are based upon a God that judges us and we are taught that if we are not good little boys and girls we will feel the wrath of God. Putting it bluntly our churchmen have taught us to fear God. Why do you think this is? Could it be that they have something to hide, like the truth? Fear is the result of withholding truth. Why would they not give us the truth? Could it be because their power and wealth is based upon keeping us ignorant and therefore enslaved to them?

It is totally understandable why the majority of people have moved away from God, or I should say, the church. It's too difficult trying to be 'good' all of the time. And how many times have you tried to do the right thing only for it to turn out wrong? You're on a loser before you start, you sinner, you! And then of course your church expects you to confess your sins to them as they say they are the only ones that have an audience with God - a lie that has served to separate you from God. The truth is, we all have a direct line to God. Are you brave enough to turn your back on religion?

Who says what is good? Who says what is bad? Who says what is right? Who says what is wrong? It is not God! God has never judged you, you have only ever judged yourself. And inevitably you will break your own moral code, never mind the Ten Commandments! So what happens then? Well, you then have to justify to yourself what it is you've done or not done, and you do so by laying the blame on someone else, thus giving your power away (It's because of what he did or because of what she did). Therein manifests guilt. And then in an effort to get rid of your guilt you give your power away again to whomever you go to for help.

All along all you needed to do to get rid of your guilt was to forgive yourself for what you thought you did wrong or realise the truth - that you never did anything wrong. How could you possibly expect to know back then what you now know?

It is foolish for us to judge ourselves based upon our past actions or lack of them. Wisdom is in part the understanding that we all make mistakes and therefore we shouldn't beat ourselves up because of them. Choosing self-forgiveness instead of having those painful, guilty feelings; is the way out of suffering.

So what is sin? Is it not that which stands between mankind and God? If anything stands between mankind and the desire to know God, is that not sinful? What does stand between mankind and God? Could it be ignorance, guilt, doubt and fear? How have we become so ignorant and fearful? Could we have learned it? Could we have been conned? Why would they con us? Could it be to enslave us for power and money? And how have they conned us? Have we not been taught that God is outside of us and that our one and only route to God is through their teachings, the one and only Son, the one and only Truth, the one and only Way? Does this not teach us from a very early age to give our power away to a perceived higher authority that really only exists in our minds? Who are the teachers? Who therefore are the real sinners?

Many moons ago when men and women first believed that God no longer existed within their beings, they were put in a most vulnerable and dangerous position, because someone else who did profess to have the 'word of God' could then dictate how they were to live, what they were to do, how they were to do it, when they were to do it; indeed, everything! This was the greatest atrocity that has ever occurred on this planet; the shifting of the power that really exists within us all to the one source, religion. This took away our uniqueness and for most people the same reality still exists today. We have been betrayed and we are going to have to find a way to forgive that.

"Religion is riddled with law; it is dogmatic, restrictive and very judgemental. And if any one thing clouds the goodness, the beauty, the intimacy, the forgiveness and the lovingness of God, it is religion" - Ramtha.

Ride with the Wind

SEPARATED FROM THE WHOLE

The next step on my journey takes me to Australia. After a short visit to Perth, I settled on Sydney's north shore. I found work promoting a range of vitamins and it was during this time that I met a very interesting young guy, about my age at the time (late twenties). He was interesting because he dressed differently from most people, more like a hippy with a whacking great big crystal around his neck!

The crystal intrigued me and he explained how he used it for healing, kinesiology and dowsing. Because I found this fascinating, he lent me a book called 'In Tune with the Infinite'. I didn't read the entire book, probably because I wasn't ready for its knowledge at the time, but I do partly remember a lovely analogy using nature to explain God being the source of all life. I cannot remember the precise detail but I will take this opportunity to share a couple of similar analogies.

The first is a simple and obvious one. It's a Christmas tree. A few years ago I was driving through my local town and at the main set of traffic lights the council had erected a most beautiful Christmas tree in readiness for the season's festivities. There must have been well over a thousand pretty lights on this tree. I pulled over and took in its beauty and began to think that maybe we, as individuals, are the bright lights; and God is the electricity source, the life force itself.

The second analogy involves the great seas. Imagine for a moment the magnitude and power of the great oceans that exist on this planet alone. And yet this planet is but a speck of dust in our galaxy and, of course, immeasurable when trying to compare it to the unlimitedness of forever. So this is a very limiting analogy. Nevertheless, try to think of God as the great seas of the world.

Now extract several droplets of seawater from the ocean. These droplets are you and I, the sons and daughters of the living cause. How do the droplets differ from the vastness of the ocean? Well, they don't differ in quality or constitution - the sea resides in them. They are, of course, the sea. They do, however, differ in magnitude. Why? Because the individual has become separated from the whole and thus weakened. What happens if we return the droplets to the sea? The individual is now, once again, indistinguishable from the whole and becomes the strength of the whole ocean.

Our separation from God is only in our own minds and is due to how we have been conditioned to think. Closing the gap and becoming 'one' with God is the seen destiny for mankind.

Ride with the Wind

KARMA IS ONLY A LIMITED TRUTH

Most of the time I spent in Sydney I shared a flat with a girlfriend, the flat being approximately three hundred yards from a Hare Krishna temple and restaurant. My girlfriend and I went and tried their food and liked it so much that we ate there regularly once a week. If you are not aware, they serve Vedic Indian food and follow a karma free diet, abstaining from all forms of meat, eggs and fish but having milk products; not as strict as vegans and more nutritious with the milk, nuts and ghee ingredients.

Anyway, I got to know the Krishna devotees very well and found them to be a very nice group of people. Like most devoutly religious people, they are fanatical about their religion and its rituals, and most of them have completely given their power away to their god, Krishna, through their devotion to him. They have confused unconditional love with devotion. They believe in the one god that can take many forms. To them, spirituality and materialism do not go hand in hand. They do not realise that this material world is just another aspect of the manifestation of spirit. So they withdraw from material life as much as possible and live in their communities. Just like other religions, they try to convert gullible people to their truth, not accepting that everyone's path in life is different.

"Devotion is born of ignorance: it does not allow change; it only allows servitude" - Ramtha.

I did, however, learn a few things from the Krishna devotees, for which I am very grateful. The first was a statement that really struck a chord with me; it hit me right between the eyes! It said, 'the beginning of spiritual realisation is the realisation that you are not a body'. This seemed to make a lot of sense to me, at the time, and has since become a reality for me. When I first read it, I went and looked at myself in the mirror and wondered what it was that stared at me from seemingly behind my eyes. If I was more than just a body then my body cannot be my true identity, so what happens to me when my body dies? Do I also die? Apparently not, according to the devotees, 'the soul of mankind is recycled through an endless chain of births and deaths'.

So what is it that survives death? If it is a soul, then what is a soul? Is it a consciousness or a collection of memorised experiences held as some form of energy? If the former, then my mind cannot be solely housed in my physical brain. If the latter, then how does this interact with my conscious mind? And what, for that matter, is a spirit? Are the soul and spirit one and the same thing? These questions would soon become a driving force in my quest for spiritual awareness. At the time of writing, I have now had about a hundred conscious out-of-body experiences (OBEs), where my mind or if you like, my conscious awareness,

Ride with the Wind

appears to be outside of my body. I will explain these experiences in as much detail as I can recall, as we continue our journey together.

The Eastern philosophy of reincarnation made a lot of sense to me. I had always felt that there was life after death. Otherwise, what would be the purpose of life? If physical death were the ending of life then life would make no sense to me. And if we accept that reincarnation is indeed a probability, then we have to concede that it is also probable that we have lived before. So where do we go to in-between lives and how long do we stay there? And do we all reincarnate or do some of us stay in the other realms of existence indefinitely? If some of us come back here, why do we do that? I have learned the answers to all these questions…

But first, back to our Eastern fanatics. They believe in the dogma called karma. This is the law that says that ever since our creation, into the material realms of existence, we have built up a negative debt or a positive credit in the eyes of God; dependent upon whether we have been good or bad men and women. They say that the reason we come back here is to balance out our bad karma with good deeds, and so clean up the indebtedness of lifetimes of shame and guilt. The problem with this theory is we can never be good enough to repay the judgement of ourselves, and so we are always in debt and a slave to our own thoughts. Please remember that God does not judge anyone! What is love can only love. **There are no bank tellers at the Bank of God issuing debit and credit balances!**

"So we come back because we started to do things in other lifetimes and didn't complete them. That is karma. Now karma is nothing to do with good and bad. It just means unfinished business" - Ramtha.

Karma is indeed a reality for those people who believe in it. Have you ever asked yourself, why do I keep doing this? It's because you haven't learned from the experience, so you keep repeating the same pattern, again and again and again - that is what reincarnation is.

"Your soul hungers for that which it has never experienced; it lacks the data from the experience. The reason you have a soul is to occupy thought, so that thought can have a basis of reality through emotion. Your soul draws to you a feeling that captivates you, to be emerged in an adventure for the purpose of gaining wisdom and a greater mind" - Ramtha.

Ride with the Wind

AN AUSSIE SHOCKER

Whilst I was living in Sydney, I worked for a large insurance company, as an agent. I had a very nice office, overlooking the harbour. My office was a part of a whole floor of offices, which went around the wall of the building and was on the third floor. The centre of the floor was open plan and included the lift area, toilets, kitchen and a shower room.

I've got a history of volatile relationships and true to form I temporarily fell out with my girlfriend. As a result, I had no accommodation to sleep in, so one of my work colleagues suggested that I borrow his sofa bed and sleep in my office until I found a permanent resolution to my situation. This I did and to my surprise I wasn't always alone in the office! One of the other agents would regularly work until the early hours of the morning because he couldn't bear to see his wife! I found this rather amusing because he was another religious preacher, telling others how to live their lives. Another agent would regularly roll up drunk and be too scared to go home to his wife! LOL

One night, however, I was alone, and it was something to be compared to a horror movie. I was in a really deep sleep when I was suddenly woken up by a loud bang. As I struggled to bring myself around I started to hear voices and more banging. I realised we had been broken into. Just then a man went running past my internal window and karate kicked the security shutters of the reception area, which was adjacent to my office. By this time I had retrieved my underpants and put them on! I literally crawled to the phone on my desk and rang the police. I spoke to an officer at the local station and I am sure he thought it was a hoax call by his seemingly slow reactions to my life-threatening situation, and his only interest being in getting my telephone number. I, of course, gave him my location, asked them to hurry and said, 'whatever you do, don't ring me back!' As soon as I had put the phone down they called back - that's the Australian police for you. You can no doubt imagine how quickly I picked up the receiver. 'we're on our way', those bright sparks said.

Well, minutes passed which seemed like hours and I could hear the gang working their way around the building, breaking into every office, getting closer to mine by the second. The guy who had karate kicked the reception shutters had abandoned his attempt and there was no sign of him or unfortunately the police!

I had to take the bull by the horns, so to speak. I opened my office door - I'd got my trousers on by now - and said, 'listen guys, you had best be going as the police are on their way'.

To my surprise it went deadly silent. The gang had obviously scarpered before

Ride with the Wind

I'd finished my mouthful! I must have frightened them just as much as they had frightened me :) The police finally arrived and informed me that they had seen four men running from the building but were unable to catch them. What's new, I thought...

The purpose of relating this true drama to you is that after the police had left, I convinced myself that the criminals would not return and amazingly I drifted back off to sleep. Then I had the first of many unusual experiences. How long I had been asleep, this second time, I do not know but I seemingly woke up and all I could hear was the drumming of the Hare Krishna mantra. I had been lying face down on my makeshift bed and now I was hovering horizontally about two feet above it! As soon as I realised this, I was instilled with fear and I was sort of thumped back into my body.

Had I been out of my body or had I been levitating? I cannot recall seeing my body. Or was it some form of illusion induced by the shock of the trauma? Whatever it was, I know it wasn't a dream, not even one of those lucid ones where you wake up in your own dream. I had had full consciousness in my immediate environment, although the environment appeared somehow altered and vague. What a strange experience.

For sometime afterwards I talked to people about my experience but I couldn't find anyone who had experienced anything similar. I felt rather isolated and I tried to forget about it but it was always there in the back of my mind. Yet another question to be answered.

Ride with the Wind

OUT-OF-BODY EXPERIENCES

I had been back in England less than a month and was living temporarily with my parents, when I was involved in a car accident on the night of my youngest brother's twenty-first birthday celebrations. My brother and I were worse for booze and we had accepted a lift home from a friend who had appeared sober to us. How could we judge in our state of being? All I remember was gaining consciousness, realising that I was lying on the underside of the roof of an overturned mini car. I saw a hole, which was a crushed rear window, and I barely managed to drag myself through it. My left leg hurt and I put my right hand to my face to reveal it was covered in blood. I could smell petrol. It had spilled all over the road and there were people talking and smoking nearby. In my daze I realised that I had been very lucky. The gods were shining on me that night. I couldn't die on my brother's birthday.

I was taken by ambulance to the local hospital. My face was cleaned and some of the glass removed from it. My leg was x-rayed and bandaged as nothing was broken, and I was sent home with strong painkillers. This began the start of some amazing experiences.

The night after the accident I struggled to get off to sleep because of the pain I was suffering. I must have finally 'drifted off' when I felt myself being dragged out of my body! I can't describe it any other way. I was going through a process of sitting up in bed in what can only be described as a slow motion action. I was consciously aware of moving into the 'sitting upright' position and yet I realised my body was still lying down :(I had full conscious awareness and could see all aspects of my bedroom and yet it again seemed somehow altered. It was like I had accessed another realm of existence parallel to this one. My return to my body was uneventful and I simply woke up.

What was happening to me and why was it happening? Was it as a result of being unconscious in the accident? This didn't seem plausible, as my previous OBE wasn't preceded by unconsciousness. Was it as a result of the shock of the accident, the severe pain or the realisation that I had had a near-death experience (NDE)? If so, do all people who experience trauma, pain or NDE's have OBE's? Or was I simply going mad? I had to find the answers to my questions. At the time I confided in a family member who flippantly said, 'perhaps you had died and had been sent back!' This was just what I wanted to hear in the confusion that already prevailed in my mind.

Because I wanted to find out more about these experiences and I had nobody to turn to with any knowledge of them, I decided to experiment on my own. I would try to self-induce the experience. During the next two to three weeks, whilst I

Ride with the Wind

still had my leg in a splint, I would go to bed at night and relax as if preparing myself for sleep. I would then 'will' this experience into being and to my amazement it happened on nearly every occasion! It was as though by using my will, I could somehow raise my vibration and leave my body...

The altered state of awareness was always the same and it always occurred in my immediate environment, my bedroom, during the twilight hours. However, my experiences did differ slightly in that sometimes I would just 'appear' out of body without memory of the dragging or slow motion effect and other times I would feel myself being sucked back into my body as if a vacuum had got me and was pulling me back to some central core deep within myself. It was as if I was attached by some kind of umbilical cord and on occasions I felt the struggle of my consciousness trying to fit back into my body; I had to kind of wriggle to get myself back in there.

I started to get a bit worried with thoughts such as, what if I can't get back into my body? And what is the purpose of all of this? And am I doing myself any harm? As these doubts had no real foundation I decided to continue with my experimentation...

There were several things that had become a reality for me. Firstly, I could 'will' this experience into being. There was no doubt about this and all I had to do was give it my full focused intent and it would happen. *This is significant because this is how we create reality - by using our thoughts and knowing for certain that they will manifes*t. Secondly, the very fact that I could exist independently from my body proved to me that I really wasn't a body and the Hare Krishna devotees were correct at least on that point.

So what am I and how is it I can see without the use of my eyes and move without the use of my physical body?

At about the same time as these experiences were occurring I was picking at a book called 'The Journey of the Soul'. From what I can remember the book was about a man who had lost his brother in World War One and during his grieving he was visited by an Indian adept who taught him about evolution and the astral realms of existence. The teacher reunited him with his brother and the two of them had many enjoyable experiences in this parallel plane of existence. The one thing that stuck out in my memory was the fact that all motion in the astral realm is via thought and conscious intent. In the astral dimension you do not have a dense physical body to slow you down. Think it and you are there!

The next time I induced an OBE I moved myself purely by thought. I literally willed myself through my bedroom door and I could feel myself move through

Ride with the Wind

the door. I could feel the vibration of the door. The door was like being slowly bathed in another frequency or density of energy. Subsequent to that I moved myself through plaster walls, brick walls and panes of glass. The only difference between each material was a slightly different sensation and the time taken to move through it. This must be to do with the density of the different materials.

Once back out in the air or ether I could move freely, a completely weightless sensation that seemed to defy gravity and time, as we know it. Several times I would find myself outside in the local street or on a rooftop wondering where to go next. The one time I took off on a journey into the local town and I found myself flying bird-like through the streets. There were no sensations of touch or smell or of coldness. But of course, these sensations pertain only to the physical body. These were no dreams - I had had full consciousness and I was able to see. I had perceived a different reality with my mind.

During another experience I flew through unrecognisable streets, tree-lined boulevards with Victorian mansions, and I remember dodging the trees and eventually arriving in a beautiful lounge via the window of course! I must admit if I were in your shoes I'd be thinking, yeah, and pigs can fly too! It is very difficult trying to relate to you an experience that I have had, which was very real for me, yet my memory of it is sketchy and bears little resemblance to this reality. Some experiences are difficult to put into words. Words often limit the expression of our thoughts.

Anyway, back to the lounge. There was an open roaring fire and I was seated on a settee. I picture a chesterfield or similar. Moreover, there were two people, beings, entities, spirits or whatever, present in the lounge. The male impression stood by the fireplace and the female sat beside me on the settee, and I got the feeling they were my deceased grandparents. I particularly remember the lady because she looked young and beautiful with long flowing hair and obviously happy to be where she was. It was as if she was saying, 'look at me now'.

I know that we conversed but I cannot remember any details of the conversation, or details of the male impression other than being aware of his presence in a dark suit. I do know that whoever they were, they presented themselves in the form and manner in which they wanted me to see them, young-looking and happy to be together. That was my impression of them.

Afterwards, something dawned on me. I had experienced a vision, a perception of reality, without the use of my physical eyes! How could this be? I had always thought that we couldn't see without the use of our eyes. Perhaps we really do see with our minds and our eyes simply allow us to view this physical reality by allowing in light to create the images in our minds. Just like the mechanics of

Ride with the Wind

photography, our eyes are the lenses and the frontal lobes of our brains are the screen. Well, this does open up a Pandora's box because it begs the fundamental question, what is reality?

Like all of you, I dream every night and I understand that these dreams are my body's way of rejuvenating itself during sleep. I have definitely improved my dream recall in recent years due to my increased awareness. Also I occasionally have what are called lucid dreams, where one wakes up in the dream, is aware of oneself intermittently or is conscious throughout the whole dream. In this state there seems to be different degrees of consciousness, different dimensions of reality and a different pliability of one's surroundings. On many occasions I **Ride with the Wind** and alter my surroundings by using my mind. As I think about objects so they instantly appear. I wish I could manifest things as quickly in this physical dimension. Perhaps I could if I learned how to conquer time…

On one occasion I was taken by another entity to a place of extreme beauty. I will try my best to describe it to you. It was a bathing or swimming arena made out of what appeared to be some kind of stone. There were large Roman-looking pillars and steps to sit upon but the most striking thing was the water. It was like crystal and it glittered with unforgettable beauty. There were many people bathing there and their appearance brings to mind the word celestial. They were aware of my presence and they didn't seem to mind my being there; they just carried on with their activities. I was left with a lasting impression of extreme beauty and love and, moreover, a belief that these other realms of existence do indeed exist.

Lastly, there are my experiences of altered consciousness that seem to occur in the dead of night and definitely in my immediate surroundings. At the time of writing, the last of such experiences occurred about a year ago. I have a habit of getting up about four in the morning to go to the toilet. As usual, or so I thought, I was heading towards the bathroom when I suddenly realised I was holding someone's hand! My immediate reaction was to get rid of it as if it was contaminated or something. I had been sleeping alone and no one else was in my flat, so there was no explanation for this happening. In the next moment, after I kind of threw the hand away, I realised that I was out of my body and I pleaded with the force that was pulling me back not to do so. I woke up and went for my pee! These experiences are now few and far between and I relish the opportunity of having them to learn further about this apparent 'other reality'.

Ride with the Wind

A LIGHT FLOATING ON A SEA OF DARKNESS

Most physicists agree that everything came from nothing in the first place. Imagine for a moment that there was a beginning of time and creation, before what we see was created. We are going back to a time before time was created and nothing existed. It does not matter whether it was fifty thousand or fifty trillion years ago. We will learn later that time, although a reality, is indeed an illusion. Now imagine looking up into the sky at night; it's a clear sky, not a cloud in sight. Furthermore, and for the first time ever, you cannot see a single star or moon. And daybreak never comes because there is no sun either. What would reality be under such conditions? Well, nothing would exist because nothing exists without light.

So there you are suspended, weightless in this velvet-black nothingness we call the void. You feel as if you have been catapulted into outer space, beyond all known galaxies, and you are free-floating in this vast nothingness without any point of reference. What would be your reality?

Well, you don't have a body, it hasn't been created yet! And so you cannot sense anything. In fact, all you have is perception, a perception of nothingness, total darkness. And although you feel that you move about, because there is no other point of reference you are really going nowhere; indeed, everywhere just IS. Without another point of reference there is no distance to anything and therefore no space, just you floating in infinity. And you have no sense of time; it simply doesn't exist without distance and space.

Why is this and what are you? You, as always, are you, consciousness and energy suspended in the void, *a light floating on a sea of darkness*. And as you are there alone with no other point of consciousness, there is no distance, space or time because these realities only exist between two or more points of consciousness. This may sound a bit heavy, please bear with me.

So what is consciousness? To explain what it is we need to take a step back, before even we existed! We are now back in the void - 'all bundled together'.

Imagine for a moment that you are lying in your bed at night with your eyes closed or with a blindfold on. You put your earplugs in and you become completely oblivious to your surroundings. You could be anywhere and everywhere. Or you take a trip to a health farm and lie in one of those floatation tanks for a few hours. What is your reality?

You've shut off all your senses and you're suspended in darkness, oblivious to everything except one thing - your own thoughts. You are floating in the void.

Ride with the Wind

The void, in order to create, has to have the potentials to create from itself, and these potentials are thoughts unawakened. To create everything it has to have all potentials. Ramtha has defined the void as **one vast nothing materially, yet all things potentially**.

Consciousness is therefore the void awakened, equating self-awareness. There can only be self-awareness if there can be a reflection of self. The void needed a face and the primal consciousness that it created from contemplating itself was its face. This point of consciousness, which exists in the cells of all life, Ramtha calls Point Zero.

This contemplative process was also the birthing of mind, the mind of God. And deep contemplation is still the best method of expanding one's mind today! When you pull an abstract thought from your subconscious mind you awaken it and it then becomes a part of the neurological network of your conscious mind. Please focus and stay with me...

What does all of this mean to you? It means that your reality is based upon your conscious mind, its perception and the perception of your bodily senses feeding it. The important point to remember is - your reality is thus different from everyone else's reality, as your perspective, your point of viewing life, is different from all other people.

No two people share the same reality and therefore no two people share exactly the same truth.

I find this most interesting because we are all living life from different points of view and we therefore have different opinions based upon our different realities and self-created values. So why do we argue with each other when our realities and values are different? Who are we to say someone else is wrong? And what gives us the right to judge something we obviously know little about? Why don't we just allow and accept that another person has their point of view instead of trying to get them to accept our reality? You are not them and so cannot live for them and they are not you and cannot live for you. This sense of ownership of reality forms part of an illusionary image we have built up around ourselves, which finds its way into our relationships with others.

Before we return to the story, let us take a quick look at what truth is. I learned from Ramtha that truth is linked to reality in that whatever your reality is, is your truth. Truth is therefore also subjective. Everyone's truth is different because everyone perceives a different reality in life. We are deity, creating our own truth.

Everyone's path in life has a different soul agenda and your path is exactly where

Ride with the Wind

you are standing right now. Where you are right now, where you live, the people in your life and how you live your life, is where you want to be otherwise you wouldn't be there! It is a reflection of where your consciousness and energy are held. What is in your life is therefore the result of your consciousness and energy. The two are inseparable. It is your reality, indeed, it is your truth. There is no ONE truth that everybody should live by - that is an enslaving dogma coming from a tyrannical consciousness.

What does all this mean? Truth like reality is not absolute. And yet we are always trying to convert other people to our truth instead of just allowing them 'to be'. We must understand that our truth and our reality are purely our perception from our point of view. We must learn to love and respect other people enough to allow them their truth and accept that their path in life is different to ours. If others want to share their opinions and points of view then that is not only all right but beneficial; it adds to our understanding of them: it adds to the whole. Moreover, we must start to live our own truth, without duality, and not give our power away to a religious mindset or try and inflict our truth upon others.

Ride with the Wind

ALL ABOARD WITH RON

When I was in my early thirties, one day I was in the city centre of Birmingham minding my own business, getting a Wimpy meal if I remember correctly, when I was approached by a very persistent young woman wanting me to go to her offices to complete some form of psychometric test. She was from the Church of Scientology and wasn't going to give in until I had said yes! I had heard a few stories about the Scientologists and preferring to formulate my own truth, I decided to play along. Anyway, I had some free time and I have always been a sucker for a salesperson!

The woman sat me down at a desk and I proceeded to answer the two-hour multiple choice questionnaire. It was like being back at school! I found some of the questions difficult to answer because of their ambiguousness and my answers very often didn't appear in the choice of answers available.

I returned a few days later to get my results and they had produced a line graph for me, grading me on a scale against various personality traits. They patted me on the back saying how well I'd done but there were a couple of areas that I was weak in, and that they were the ones that could help. Here we go again, hook, line and sinker! They encouraged me to read a short book on Dianetic co-auditing, not realising that I'd already read L. Ron Hubbard's best-selling book Dianetics, The Science of Mental Health. I played along until they tried to get me to pay for an auditing course, which is a type of counselling course working with one's own mental image pictures. I had to convince them that I was financially broke to get myself off the hook. Anyway, I had an ulterior motive.

Brian, my hypnotherapy tutor, had a friend who had been a Scientologist for many years, and when his friend resigned from the 'org', they apparently hounded him relentlessly. One is not supposed to leave the 'org'. Over the years he had told Brian about an instrument that Hubbard had created, which was described to me as an advanced form of lie detector. Brian had used it in association with his friend and he explained to me how useful it was for pinpointing 'blocked energy' in a person's past. By wiring a person up to the machine and taking them back into their past time line, the machine can locate by registering a 'charge', a traumatic event or an event where the person has broken their own moral code. And then, by using a series of precise questions, the charge can be released thus releasing the person from their own judgement of themselves. This is evidenced by the needle on the machine flowing freely and the heightened state of 'tone' achieved by the individual.

To cut a long story short, I would just like to share with you that I had many meetings with a lady who is (was) one of the top Scientologists in the world, and

Ride with the Wind

was at one time very close to their leader, Ron Hubbard. On her visits to Birmingham, the lady and I would spend many hours chatting about world conditions, tyrants and conspiracies and she would help me with Scientology auditing using the E-meter. I can vouch that the meter, in the hands of a skilled operator, is a useful tool in helping a person to get rid of their emotional baggage. In fact, it is a brilliant 'confessional' tool because the meter is somehow sensitive to our thoughts, the mental image pictures that we store as memories. It is said that 'confession is good for the soul' and that certainly has been my experience with this machine.

To try to understand how the machine works I would like to refer you back to the paragraphs on 'what is reality'. Ramtha teaches that consciousness and energy have both come from the void, a sleeping inert medium of never ending potential, and that they are inextricably combined. Consciousness is the thought potential awakened and energy is the thought or now consciousness in motion. They are inseparable. This means that all consciousness has energy and all energy has consciousness. When you slow consciousness and energy down you get light and when you lower it further you eventually get electrons and positrons and subsequently solid-appearing mass. When a person holds a couple of electrodes connected to a sophisticated meter, their thought energy can be measured by an electrical charge. Moreover, a change in that energy can be seen on the needle of a properly calibrated machine.

Before I leave the Scientologists, I would like to mention that during my discussions with 'the lady', I asked her opinion on what mind is and how it relates to the body and spirit. She told me that mind is not confined to the brain, that people should stop thinking in purely physical terms, and that the spirit carries the mind around like a handbag! This suggests that our minds are non-local and probably therefore simply an accumulation of our consciousness, the sum total of our knowingness.

This now begs the question, what is the spirit? She continued to tell me that the purpose of auditing was to bring a person to a state of 'clear', where they had owned or conquered their mental aberrations, which I interpreted as meaning their judgement of themselves. After becoming 'clear', they go on to the higher levels of attainment, which are called OT levels. OT is short for Operating Thetan, Thetan being Hubbard's word for the Spirit. They have a gradient scale of achievement through their various levels of spiritual development.

The Scientologists wanted me to join an elite group of members known as the 'Sea Org'. They are the ones with the highest IQ's and thus considered to have the most potential. This was a big decision for me at the time and I researched it thoroughly.

Ride with the Wind

I had the pleasure of visiting their headquarters at Saint Hill near East Grinstead. I was impressed with the set-up and the way things were run. I looked into their various charters, rules and regulations, and code of ethics. I can report that they have the highest ethical and moral values, that they believe man to be basically good and that their purpose is to free man from the chains that bind him. They told me that there were suppressive forces at work on this planet, which also involved alien species from other galaxies, and that my salvation lay in my own hands and my ability to attain the OT levels of evolvement.

I agree with them but also see how they will never attain the 'highest' levels because of their devotion to their leader, a man who failed to become a master.

My experience of Scientology was a useful interlude on my journey of self-discovery, but it is far from being the whole answer to one's enlightenment.

Ride with the Wind

EVERYTHING IS SPIRITUAL IN ITS OWN WAY

I had become interested in matters of the Spirit and for some time I had been meaning to check out my local Spiritualist church. I think my procrastination was due to the fact that I had grown to dislike church establishments. I was assured by a friend that the Spiritualists were different, so I went along to experience their church-type service.

The first thing I noticed was a picture on the wall of a pair of hands radiating light. I took this to mean the healing hands of a Christ. It was obviously open to individual interpretation. There was an emblem on another wall that said something about truth and light. I sat in the rectangular hall. I must admit it didn't feel like church at all; people were chatting and joking and laughing! There was a full congregation; in fact the church was jam-packed. Whilst I sat there I picked up the hymn book and read the seven principles of Spiritualism on the inside cover. To my surprise I found very little dogma and I agreed with all of them except one. As these principles are left open to an individual's interpretation, I found that I was sitting most comfortably.

During the service we sang hymns and sang the so-called Lord's Prayer with a few alterations to the Christian wordings. About fifty per cent of the service was devoted to a medium, a psychic, who communicated messages to people in the audience from their departed loved ones. The shock on some of the people's faces at being chosen and the meaningful nature of the messages being delivered, further convinced me about life after death and the interconnectedness of all life.

I visited the Spiritualist church for about a year in total and I can report that they provide evidence consistently of life after death. They also help people with hands-on and absent healing, free of charge too! I found them to be some of the nicest people I have ever met. I did an 'awareness' course with them, which although serious in nature, was great fun. We would sit around and do simple exercises, like looking for and feeling a person's aura, which they said was a precursor for one who wishes to become involved in healing. And we would try to develop our psychic abilities by reading each other's thought-forms or holding an object and knowing everything about it. It was all good fun but not too enlightening for me.

As is typically the case with most awareness-type groups that I have participated in, the groups are normally only receptive to conversation that fits in with their own limited viewpoints. Anyone who has a different viewpoint or who stands out in the flock is not wanted because they are seen as a threat to the image consciousness of the group. It is then a case of 'your energy isn't quite right for this group' or 'your energy is too strong'.

Ride with the Wind

It is so important in any group situation to have guidance from one who is open-minded, who is comfortable with a diverse range of people's awareness and who is sufficiently evolved not to feel threatened by another's viewpoint. In other words, the leadership should understand the purpose and objective of the group; their role in the group and admit when their knowledge is lacking. The group should not be run to reinforce the image of the group leader but rather to provide a forum where members can contemplate new ideas and thus expand themselves.

The last occasion I went to the Spiritualist church I was accompanied by my uncle who had previously had the same experience some ten years earlier. On this occasion my deceased grandfather, my uncle's father, was channelled through the medium. It was pleasant hearing the message that came through for my uncle and the childhood memories that the medium was bringing forth for him. This evidence was very close to home and it was a nice thought that **no one is ever lost in God's kingdom.**

After that night I became a little closer to my uncle. We found that we had at least one thing in common, matters of the spirit, that some call paranormal or supernatural. I suppose I was ready to take the next step on my path when my uncle suggested I read a book called The Celestine Prophecy. The book is about a man who goes to Peru in search of nine insights of wisdom and the insights prove to be a great encouragement to him on his journey.

The first insight talks about synchronicity, the so-called coincidences that happen to us all. For a long time, I had thought that coincidences were some kind of universal force that brought people together for specific learning experiences, and this was the teaching of this insight. Another insight talked about the power struggles that exist in certain relationships and how people compete for each other's energy. Well, I think we can all relate to that one! The insight that appealed to my imagination the most, described how an ancient civilisations had collectively evolved to a point where they, as spiritual beings, had mastered their illusions and ascended to the heavens; leaving no trace of any footprints behind. In other words, they had somehow raised their body frequencies and taken their bodies with them!

My quest for knowledge continues as always. One day I was browsing in a local bookstore when a book called 'The Truth in the Light' jumped off the shelf at me. It's a book that has been compiled by a nationwide organisation, which collated information on near-death experiences, from about eight hundred letters received. If my memory serves me correctly, about five hundred of the letters were useful to them and they proceeded to look for common occurrences in each near-death experience.

Ride with the Wind

Some very interesting facts came to light. Most people reported that during the experience they travelled through a kind of tunnel towards a brilliant light, whilst being encompassed in a feeling of absolute love. Some met their loved ones and others talked about 'beings of light'. Some of them made it to the light and still held in this absolute love, they underwent a 'light review', where their life was replayed to them like replaying a reel of film at high speed. Of just as much interest to me was the fact that no less than two-thirds of respondents reported being out of their bodies prior to going through the tunnel of love. At last! I now had some hard evidence that I wasn't going crazy! The other interesting factor was that most of them said life had become more precious to them because they now knew there was no such thing as death. They were now viewing death as an illusion and life through new eyes - beautiful.

Now what have OBE's got to do with NDE's? Well, at the point of death of our bodies, our consciousness, or dare I say our spirit, pulls away and leaves the body. But what is the difference therefore between actual death, near death and being out of body? The answer has to do with what the tunnel is and that which is journeying through it.

Ramtha describes the actual moment of bodily death as painless and taking but a moment; it is like going to sleep! The spirit pulls away from the body (hence the OBE) and calls forth its child. The soul travels through the body's energy seals, giving the effect of the tunnel of love, and goes towards the light. It leaves the body through the crowning seventh seal, which is the light that is seen. You are then in a state of pure emotion where everything is amplified and intensified. The moment life ebbs from your body, you are in another embodiment of your spirit and your final embodiment depends entirely upon your level of consciousness; the level of mind you have realised from your journey here.

On a couple of occasions I have made reference to the body's aura or auric field. This is actually an energy field of light that exists around your body and every one of its cells. It is the force field that keeps your body together and stops it from just dispersing into the atmosphere! Your body cannot exist without the light that surrounds it and holds it together. Not only can some of us see this light but more importantly, its existence has been proven scientifically with the use of Kirlian photography. This light is consciousness and energy that has manifested itself as various bodies of light comprising your spirit and soul.

The Ramtha book, 'A Beginner's Guide to Creating Reality' gives detailed information on how spirit, soul and the bodies that comprise one's aura, came into being.

Ride with the Wind

Here is a brief explanation of the seven levels, as taught at Ramtha's school of Enlightenment:

1. The first level represents the physical plane and is below conscious awareness.

2. Social consciousness is represented by the infrared body in the infrared realm.

3. Awareness is represented by the light body in the visible light realm.

4. Bridge consciousness is represented by the ultraviolet blue body of Shiva.

5. Super consciousness is represented by the golden body in the x-ray realm.

6. Hyper consciousness is represented by the colour rose and gamma rays.

7. Ultra consciousness (Christ consciousness) is colourless and is represented by infinite unknown (faster than gamma rays).

Actual death of the body occurs when the soul permanently leaves it. The near-death experience (NDE) is where the soul starts its journey through the body's seals and returns, or if it leaves the body it returns very quickly. The OBE is simply the spirit, as mind (the individuals mind), becoming free from the body; but the soul remains close to or in the body.

Once again a greater explanation of this can be realised by reading the Ramtha book 'A Beginner's Guide to Creating Reality'.

Ride with the Wind

MY WEIRD FRIEND EUWEN

A business opportunity led me back to Australia to help launch a new company at the forefront of incentive programmes and smart card technology. I was housed in a company apartment sharing with an Australian man named Euwen. Shortly after arriving I found that my energy levels had become incredibly high, so much so that I couldn't sleep for three days! I telephoned my uncle in the UK and he suggested that I was 'in the flow' and definitely living 'in tune' with my soul. Whatever the explanation was, I sure felt a lightness of being and a desire to engage this new business opportunity.

I got to know Euwen quite well during the four months I remained in Aussie. He was the strangest man I'd ever met. He was obviously knocking on in years, not because of his appearance but due to the fact that he had a grown-up family. I couldn't hazard a guess at his age but he must have been at least in his early fifties. We were both working from the same office in Sydney and on occasions I would walk with him to work. I am almost ashamed to admit that I struggled to keep up with his pace of walking. He had a vitality and zest for life that I'd not encountered before. He would work tirelessly all day, sometimes as long as eighteen hours, writing the computer software for the company. At weekends, if he had any time off, he would either get the train to Melbourne to oversee his interest in another business or he would just take off for a long walk. Sometimes he would be gone for two days and walk around forty miles! Quite a feat for a man who was actually in his mid-sixties at the time.

Euwen and I became good friends. I've always got on better with people who others find weird. It is one of the fundamental laws of the universe - like attracts like! The one day I wanted Euwen's opinion on something and when I asked what he thought, he said, 'I don't think' and gave me one of his hypnotic gazes. I knew there was something I could learn from this man. I observed that although he was an intellectual man he also had a simplicity about him that bordered on genius, a rare combination.

At the end of each day, he would return to the apartment, pour himself a large Scotch, smoke a couple of cigarettes and retire to his bedroom to read his Carlos Castaneda books. He was a student of the teachings of Don Juan, the great sorcerer as written about by Castaneda.

Then one night I caught him. I had gone to the gym after work and he had gone home early for some reason. I must have returned earlier than he had expected for he was doing a strange blowing exercise, standing in the middle of the lounge. I am a very worldly person and accordingly I took no notice of him but he must have been slightly embarrassed because he stopped what he was doing and

Ride with the Wind

proceeded to explain. He had a large manual on the dining table headed 'The Teachings of Don Juan' and he was performing simple exercises from it.

We sat opposite each other across the dining table and as he spoke to me I could see a greenish coloured light emanating from his head and then I noticed it encompassed his whole being, reaching out about three inches from his body. I was kind of fixated on his being, looking at part of his aura and entranced by the words he spoke. He said that some of the exercises were like initiate tests and that when he had mastered one he would then move on to the next. At that time he was perfecting his vision and he was practicing by standing on the balcony of the apartment and focusing on a tree about a half-mile away. He claimed he was able to send his vision down a kind of tunnel into the leaves of the tree. He could see the intricate detail inside each leaf!

Astonished as I was, I had no reason to disbelieve him, because I knew him to be a thoroughly genuine man. Our conversation finished by him telling me that he was affiliated with a group of initiates elsewhere in Australia and that their final test was to throw themselves off a cliff and defy death! In other words, they were to disappear into the wind like some of our ancient civilisations had done before them. He likened this to Yeshua's final initiate test. Jesus had to undergo physical death and then using the power of his will, he had to resurrect his already decaying body. We all know that he succeeded in doing this and thus he became a Christ.

Ride with the Wind

BUTT HEADS WITH THE RAM

The business opportunity in Australia didn't work out and I returned to England after just four months. One day as I was driving home from my city centre office, I decided to drop by and visit my uncle for a coffee. I had cause to see him. When I got there he was playing with his new toy, the Internet. Whilst he was engrossed in his searches, I browsed his bookshelves that lined the walls of his home office. A white book seemingly jumped off one of the shelves; it was entitled Ramtha - the White book. I flicked through the book and found myself reading a chapter called 'Life after Life'. I was gripped; I couldn't put the book down! Fortunately, after some persuasion, my uncle lent it to me. It was and is the most enlightening book I have ever read. In addition, because of my interest, my uncle printed details off the Internet about Ramtha's School of Enlightenment. I read the book and the Internet details with eagerness and requested an information pack from the school in Yelm, Washington.

A couple of weeks later I received a colour folder and brochure detailing the activities of the school and the achievements of some of their advanced students. Due to reading the White Book, the basic details on the Internet and the school's marketing literature, everything was starting to make sense to me. I was definitely back on track and my soul was rejoicing! Amongst the list of student abilities were the abilities of psychic awareness, manifestation, out-of-body experiences and miraculous healings. I instantly booked myself on the next beginner's course!

The school is also known as the American Gnostic School and is run along the lines of the Ancient Schools of Wisdom that existed in the times of Jesus and the early centuries a.d.. Gnosticism is about gaining knowledge through personal experience and the acceptance that our salvation, indeed our power, lies within us. It is not about religion, faith, belief or giving our power away to others. It is about *knowing* not guesswork or blind faith.

The event was scheduled for spring 1997. I was now on a flight to Seattle heading into unknown territory. I had arranged accommodation and was to be picked up from the airport by a student associated with the school, which is affectionately known as RSE. A rusty old brown Cadillac pulls up and out gets Elizabeth, a lady in her sixties, her long grey hair in a pigtail and wearing track pants, a sweat shirt and clogs. We exchanged courtesies and my bags got thrown in the boot!

I found Yelm to be a small laid-back town and it reminded me of a suburb of Auckland. I was definitely in hill-billy country; it was like a time warp to the past. Elizabeth's house is sheltered from the road behind evergreen trees and set in about five acres of beautiful virgin land. It is left to nature except for cutting the grass and a few modifications to her dwelling.

Ride with the Wind

I was most impressed when I discovered that she is a completely sovereign entity. She supplies her own lighting and heating from solar energy panels and a generator. She supplies herself with hot and cold water pumped from a well. She provides an income for herself and she has made 'rainy day' provisions for many years to come. I queried her about her lifestyle and the provisions she had made. She responded, 'you'll learn about the days that are coming at the ranch (RSE)'.

After a couple of days rest, to recover from the jet lag, Elizabeth drove me to the ranch for my beginners' event - level one. The setting is a large beautifully converted horse stables amongst forty acres of fields and woodland. Every amenity is catered for, including a well-stocked annex selling books and tapes.

The next forty-eight hours had a marked effect upon my life. I had previously witnessed psychics and trance mediums and even a psychic surgeon who had channelled a two hundred year old doctor, but never before had I witnessed a thirty-five thousand year old male energy being channelled through a female body. Incredible! Ramtha stood there in the body of JZ Knight for two days and gave us over twenty hours of the most wonderful teachings on the nature of reality. He addressed the subject without notes or hesitation and gave us a polished monologue of ancient wisdom beyond measure or value. Absolutely awesome!

Part of the philosophy I learned has since, through my own realisations, become a truth for me; and I have done my best to share some of it with you in this book.

Proceeding level one, at that time, was a day interval and then the beginners' event - level two, started. This was a six-day retreat and not all of the people made it to level two. This has nothing to do with any lack of qualification or any failure on their part; as there are no qualifications for entry and you cannot fail the school: you can only quit.

In my opinion, the day interval served the purpose of weeding out the intellectuals from the potential geniuses. The intellectuals tend to always complicate issues. They are complex individuals who cannot accept a simple truth even when it's staring them in the face. We have some outstanding intellectual minds on this planet and their ability to regurgitate rhetoric is unquestionable. However, intellectual minds have made simplicity a mystery, showing how powerful they are in their state of absolute pompousness. It is a fact that intellectual people rarely accomplish single feats of genius. It takes a simple mind to comprehend genius. A genius is one who has the ability to captivate simplicity, not complicate it.

My level-two retreat was a combination of teachings from Ramtha and simple but powerful practical exercises performed by the students under Ramtha's guidance. There was no discipline too difficult or too demanding. People of all

Ride with the Wind

ages and all degrees of physical dexterity frequent the school. Many languages are interpreted there.

I feel that it is important that I share with you my experiences as a student rather than detail the activities of the school in general. For those of you who are interested to know more about the activities of the school, I would recommend that you get a book called Finding Enlightenment by J. Gordon Melton. This is a comprehensive, objective study of Ramtha's School of Enlightenment by a man who chronicles new age and new religious movements and who spent two years at the school, as a student, attending both beginners and advanced events. Ironically, Melton is a devout christian, an ordained elder in a methodist church.

My experiences at RSE are too many to list here. However, of all the exercises taught, the one that I perceive I have derived the most benefit from, is called Consciousness and Energy breathing or just C&E for short. I cannot describe this discipline to you in great detail. My words would only limit your understanding of it. It is suffice to say that it is a breathing exercise done seated and wearing a blindfold. Ramtha developed C&E whilst convalescing on a rock and it was this exact process that he used to burn away his altered-ego (image-consciousness) and ascend in the presence of his people some thirty-five thousand years ago. He tells us that he was the first person to ascend from this planet.

The first time I did C&E I raised my kundalini energy to such an extent that I found myself in the void and felt the incredible love our Father has for all of us. In that moment, I had a realisation and was filled with emotion. How could I have ever judged anyone when God has never judged me? How can anyone judge something they know so little about? How can God judge if he is all things to all men? He would be judging himself! He loves us all equally. No one is superior or inferior in his eyes. If we judge another then we are really judging ourselves.

My reference to God in the masculine infers both genders because God is neither gender and both. A woman is a man with a womb.

God mirrors us all perfectly. We were made in his image. We are the ones who choose to view God, to view life, imperfectly. We need to realise that we have a symbiotic relationship with our Father. We are the creators and he is the source of our creations. We are indeed the apple of his eye and he is our loving Father.

At the same event, during another C&E session, I was focusing on the word 'wisdom' and so intent was my focus that I saw a plume of feathers emerge from my head and I became the wise Red Indian Chief; sitting and watching his tribe dancing around the camp fire. I can only describe the experience as a vision, which I held and enjoyed for several minutes. I did not imagine it. I saw it and

Ride with the Wind

became it, and I felt the serenity of one who is wise. To have had such a vision, especially whilst wearing blindfolds, was an incredible experience for me.

Many students at RSE report miraculous healings and others, like myself, have been healed only to reaffirm an old reality by looking in a mirror or doubting what had occurred. Our reality is always how we see it as the observer. This 'observer principle' has been verified by scientists, who have observed the effects of consciousness on the movement of photons of light. Our consciousness affects our emotional make-up, which in turn affects our physical bodies.

The increase in conscious awareness experienced by practicing C&E, is the result of raising your energy to attract 'higher' thought frequencies, which cause realisations to occur whilst in session and in the days that follow. C&E takes you to where your subconscious and conscious minds marry and become one. This is where you experience 'being in the now'. All knowledge is then available to you because all knowledge exists in the now moment.

My second visit to Yelm was during the autumn of 1997. This was a three-day follow-up event known, at the time, as beginners' - level three. This was an intense yet light-hearted few days, which involved a combination of disciplines, eloquent teachings from Ramtha and a celebration with red wine, pipe tobacco, bread and cheese. It was a most enjoyable event and one that would change my life.

After the wine evening I found myself in the arms of a young woman, another of Ramtha's students. Nothing unusual, you may think, after a few glasses of wine and with my track record for the ladies! However, this was different. I wasn't being passionate, I was sobbing and it continued for most of the night and I didn't know why. The next day I spoke with some of the other students and one of them suggested that it was the start of the *dark night of the soul*. When I asked about this, I was told that it is when your darkest days beseech you and you start to become purified by way of your energy returning back to you through your emotional body. The energy carries with it the emotions that previously somebody else was the target of.

On my return to England, I realised that God had become the most important aspect in my life. After all, what is God not? I wanted to become more genuine and start to look at my life more openly and evenly. I realised that this would mean that certain people, places and things would go out of my life, and that my future was definitely now in the realms of the unknown. I could no longer hold the old energy together and live in the past like most people do. I had to go forward, I had passed the point of no return. This was going to make me unpopular in some quarters, but I knew I was gradually moving beyond social consciousness and had to start to live and speak my truth.

Ride with the Wind

In the springtime of 1998, I completed my fourth event as part of Ramtha's secondary group. It was eight days in duration and the focus was on Blue Body healing. It is beyond the scope of this book to even attempt to explain this to you and, in any event, it is something you need to experience for yourself. What I would like to share with you is another experience I had whilst engaged in C&E, which was very liberating for me.

When I was ten years of age I lost my innocence to an older boy. Amongst other things we engaged in sodomy and the next day the boy bragged to me that he had also had sex with my next door but one neighbour, an eleven-year-old girl. At the time I didn't really understand what had happened and there was certainly no one I could talk with about it. I started to think there was something wrong and that I must be some kind of sexual pervert, although I didn't really know what that was. My parents had bought my younger brother and I a set of Encyclopaedia Britannica to help us with our school work, and I used to spend time reading up on my condition - sexual perversion. As you would expect, I didn't get any answers from the encyclopaedias and as I grew up and became a teenager, I withdrew more and more into my shell of guilt.

I conveniently forgot about the situation but I always knew that it had affected me. I thought that I had dealt with it during my E-meter sessions with the Scientologists but apparently the justification of being an innocent child at the time was not enough. I was still bearing the emotional scars.

During the C&E session, after a chain of associated events had come to mind, to my surprise, the situation arose. As I relived those past holographic images, I realised that my friends and I were all gods playing and I loved them all, including the older boy concerned. The older boy had simply been experiencing adolescence and had used his influence over his younger playmates. Now here is the crucial bit. I had judged what had happened and as a result had lost my ability to love. Because of my judgement of the situation, I was no longer seeing the perfection of life, just the imperfection. I now had another pearl of wisdom, which released me from that past situation.

Since that time I have heard Ramtha say that many of us have experienced such happenings but have never admitted to ourselves that we actually enjoyed the experiences. It is better that we reveal the truth about these self-judgements than keep them hidden and festering within.

It is only when we resolve our emotions neurologically, as wisdom, that we are free of them and thus free of our past. Christ is born of a virgin means that Christ consciousness is virgin territory, untainted by an unresolved emotional past.

Ride with the Wind

THE JOURNEY OF YOUR SOUL

We have already talked about how at the point of bodily death the spirit pulls away from the body in order to rejuvenate itself. Hence you have the out-of-body experience because you are the spirit that pulls away. As I have said earlier, you don't have to die to experience the freedom of your true self. You can be in another universe and be in touch with your soul, feeding it with information from your adventures into the unknown. The spirit is the communicator, which is never more than a moment away and the soul is its scribe. Actual bodily death occurs when the spirit calls forth the soul and the soul leaves through what appears to be a tunnel of light. It is, in fact, you, your soul, which is love, moving through the bodily seals to exit the body. The body is then left with just its cellular genetic memory and this facilitates the process of its decay.

So what happens next and where do we go to? Ramtha has given a beautiful series of teachings on life between lives, entitled The Planes of Bliss, which are available on CD. Below I will summarise but I encourage you to listen to the whole series.

When you first immersed yourself into this physical realm, your soul fractured due to the polarisation from lowering your energy into mass. Imagine for a moment a Terry's Chocolate Orange. When opened it fractures into pieces. All of the emotions you have experienced in the human drama have come from pure love in the first place. They are the pieces of chocolate orange. How could you truly know unconditional love without experiencing and owning the emotions of hatred, anger, resentment, jealousy etc.? What you need to do is put the pieces of the orange back together and become whole again.

As Ramtha explains, we accomplish this whilst we're on a Plane of Bliss by intricately planning our next incarnation, to give us the ideal circumstances in which to learn what it is our soul is lacking. The 'pieces' that we lack are nothing more than wisdom that we can only get from our experiences, the realisation is a feeling that the soul captures as emotion; and we can only get this emotional experience through having the senses of a physical body. Whatever destiny we create for ourselves on a Plane of Bliss, we cannot realise it there because we need the physical body to experience it emotionally, to get the pearls of wisdom.

Ramtha teaches that your body and its genetic propensities are what you need to show you what business you need to finish up in this lifetime. Your thoughts and your emotions will tell you what you have yet to own. You don't need to be regressed into past lives or have astrology charts done because all of the answers you are seeking are staring you right in the face!

Ride with the Wind

We have now looked at death and what happens in between lives and why we are all stuck on the wheel of reincarnation. To complete this topic let us now take a look at what happens at birth:

Most parents cannot even begin to entertain the idea that their children are very old maturing souls and that their kids may have been their parents in previous lives or will be their great grandparents in their next life. Perhaps if they could comprehend and accept this, they would treat their siblings with more respect...

The fact that souls aren't finishing their unfinished business here means they can be drawn back to the same genetic line, lifetime after lifetime. This is because the family genetics offers them the same encumbrances, the same emotions, the same potentials, the ideal circumstances for completion. Here we go yet again!

According to Ramtha, the soul is placed within the seed and the egg upon conception, but the spirit, which is the caretaker of the soul, has the ability to reject the embryo at any time whilst it is forming; or even to wait for up to twelve months after birth before it takes hold of the body. When the sperm and egg come together, if the formation is not according to the will and design of the spirit, who shall control the body, the spirit will recall the soul from the body and allow it to die. At other times the spirit sees changes in the relationship between its biological parents and realises that the new conditions will not give it the best environment to experience what it needs to experience for its growth. That is the free will of the incoming spirit and why some miscarriages and cot deaths occur.

Sadly, most people never leave a legacy or make a difference in life. They just suck air until the day they die. They are victims of their parents who are victims of their parents. The sins of the parents are visited upon the children, meaning that children 'pick up' genetically the unresolved emotional patterns of their parents at the time of conception. This is not a curse but a genetic match for the incoming soul.

One of the main reasons we have stayed 'chained to the yoke' and stuck on the wheel of reincarnation; is our relationships with our fellow brothers and sisters. We have failed to understand that what we judge in another is really a mirror image of the wisdom we lack in ourselves. Close relationships can only be held together whilst the two parties mirror aspects of themselves to each other. Two people can only hold the energy together whilst they are aspiring to, and living at, similar levels of consciousness. 'We're not on the same wavelength' is a common saying that is rooted in truth.

Ride with the Wind

CINEMA 2000

Just around the corner from where I am now living, they have built a new cinema that is bigger than any I have previously seen. Do you remember when we were kids and a gang of us would go to the flicks? Great fun, eh! Let's go and check out this new cinema - I've heard it's a bit different from other cinemas.

As the usher shows us to our seats, the first noticeable difference is that it is pitch-black in there. The picture house is jam-packed and she takes us to the front row, as these seem to be the only seats available. She then says something strange that none of us could understand at the time. She says, 'everybody starts off sitting in the front row'. Anyway, we pick up the 3D glasses and we all sit there watching this movie called 'The Human Drama'.

Please try to picture this. You are sitting there watching this very dramatic movie when suddenly you spot your image in the picture! You can't believe it. So you get out of your seat and walk up to the screen and you are literally sucked into the screen and become your image in the movie. You are now in the 'human drama' with no memory of ever being in the cinema! And you're having a whale of a time. There are bodies everywhere! There are new bodies coming into the drama and old ones leaving it, and in your ignorance you conclude that this is the only reality there is.

Every so often, because of your interaction with your new environment, you get in touch with your feelings and become emotional. When this happens you are temporarily out of the picture and sitting in a seat on the second row. You notice that all of the seats on the second row are labelled with the emotion you are experiencing, and some of them are very comfortable indeed; especially the ones that serve you well. Most of the other seats on the second row are not so comfortable, in fact, they are very hard but you can't get back into the drama until you've experienced sitting in them. Poor you! All of that self-inflicted pain and suffering. And you've got to experience the second row to understand life.

You find that you are constantly going back and forth from the first to the second row and that these two rows are closely related. You are gradually becoming socially conscious and although you are still embroiled in body consciousness to the point that you are just like a machine at times, you are starting to wonder why you keep ending up in the same seats on the second row. Could it be that they are really offering you a teaching but you are refusing to learn and move on? You do not accept the wisdom from the seat so you keep coming back to it for another go. As painful as it is, you are your own worst enemy at times. Only when you get the pearls of wisdom do you free yourself from your emotional entanglements. Only knowledge can dissipate the fear and liberate you from your emotional cage.

Ride with the Wind

After many lifetimes being the butcher, the baker and the candlestick maker, you realise that there has always been somebody else pulling your strings. You have taken the step from being just a participant in life to becoming an 'observer' too. You decide that you want to be pulling some of the strings and manipulating parts of the drama. You have become more aware and you are no longer just a bag of emotional, chemical reactions. Your consciousness is now seated on the third row of seats, known as the power row. There are many roles to play on the Power row, from an Administrative Supervisor to 'King Rat', head of the World Bank. You notice that most of the seats are already filled and that you are sitting amongst the most powerful people. Once you graduate to the Power row, it is only the degree of power over others that differentiates the players in the game.

The Power row is not about power seated in you but is about power over others. If you don't know the difference then it is worth pondering that one.

Now that you are seated in the Power row you start to become more objective about life but your viewpoint is still very limited and you still slip back into the first two rows at times. So with your newly found power you think you have the best of this world because you know no other reality. You can control and participate with the body-conscious ignorance on the first row and when your plans aren't working out, you can jump back into the second row. You are coexisting in all three dimensions and what a roller coaster it is! Sadly, and one of the reasons the Power row is nearly always full, is because most of these 'death rowers' are not aware that a fourth, fifth, sixth and seventh row exist! They can only see three rows of seats in the cinema and so their ultimate personal development is epitomised by the most powerful seat. They get stuck in a different seat each lifetim; it is the wheel of reincarnation and is recycled ignorance.

Fortunately, you are very different. Although you cannot see a fourth row, you have a desire within you to want to know more and you start to question. Your quest for new knowledge becomes important to you and eventually becomes a priority in your life. You are now moving out of ignorance into enlightenment. Your consciousness is bridged between two worlds and without knowing it; you are fastly approaching the point of no return. You are still participating in your 'old' world, playing out your drama, but you have now become the observer and you are viewing life more objectively. Your consciousness is moving to a New World. You are sitting in the Power row, spending hours in contemplation, when the usher appears from behind you saying, 'can I help you?'

From the moment you first came into the cinema you knew there was more to this person, so you question her to try to reveal her disguise. 'Who are you? What are you? And where did you just come from?'

Ride with the Wind

Her reply startles you. 'I am you, I am a Master and we have seats reserved on rows four, five, six and seven! Just as you have experienced coexisting in the first three levels of life so you coexist in another four dimensions. The only difference is that you are currently not aware of yourself existing in these other dimensions because your power is seated in the lower seats, which are not representative of your true self but is a self-created Phantom-self.'

She leaves you to ponder this. How is this possible? How could I exist in other dimensions of life without knowing it? It must be some kind of latent memory, which means I have been there before! So you start to think in terms of how do I get back to recapture that true aspect of myself? As you contemplate and go deep within yourself the usher appears again and she gets bombarded with questions! You almost expected the answer: seek and ye will find, knock on the door and it will be opened. Fortunately, our usher is going to save you a lot of time searching for knowledge.

She starts to explain. 'There is plenty of room on the fourth row because no one is competing for seats. In fact, competition doesn't exist there. The fourth plane is the realm of unconditional love, which means to occupy a seat there you have to learn to love yourself and all others unconditionally. This sounds like a tall order but in fact is a natural occurrence for one who has owned the wisdom of all the seats on the first three rows.'

She shines her torch on the first row to reveal many different types of seats and therefore different roles in the human drama. It's as if each seat has its own mini-projector and as you sit in each one you get a different 3D viewpoint of the same drama. In actual fact you are creating the drama from your seat, as the screen is just showing the image from *your* projector! It is one big hologram created by millions of projectors.

You are in awe at the magnitude of the task when to your relief she explains that you have already gained most of the wisdom from the first row during your many incarnations here. 'You returned in this life with a *soul agenda* and you have completed most of your *unfinished business* here. To clean up you have to become in tune with yourself and trust and follow your instincts. Spirit will guide you to your correct seat at your stage of self-development. Your soul will press you for the learning experiences, to experience the emotions and capture them as wisdom. This is why all experiences are purposeful and never wrong; they can all amount to pearls of wisdom if coupled with lofty philosophy.'

There is a difference between an emotional feeling coming from a 'triggered' past event and an intuitive feeling urging you for a new experience. Both feelings are equally important, as we shall now see by taking a closer look at the second row.

Ride with the Wind

This is your Emotional Body. She shines her torch to reveal the full spectrum of emotions. We have the widest range and strongest emotions of any race in our galaxy. Masters are entities who have conquered themselves; they are the master of their emotions, not simply the effect of them.

This is a biggie because not only do you have to free yourself from your unfinished business here on Earth but you also have to unchain yourself from an altered way of thinking that has been created by your interaction with your environment; and this has become your living image, a great illusion, indeed: a Phantom existence which masks your true self.

You first need to look at the polarities caused by the conditioning you have been subjected to, and the resulting emotions. This involves some work on your part and is best done with a confidant. The two of you get together when you can both spare a couple of hours, at a venue where you will not be disturbed. Get plenty of paper and make four lists, as follows: -

1. The personality traits you like in other people.
2. The personality traits you dislike in other people.
3. The personality traits you like in yourself.
4. The personality traits you dislike in yourself.

This is not a time for you to use your intellect to prove how clever you are but a time for you to confront yourself and be brutally honest. Take your time to do the lists; it is a very revealing exercise. Now sit opposite one another and take it in turns to explain the reasons for your likes and dislikes. It is important that the one listening does exactly that: listens without interruption or the passing of any judgement. Try to maintain eye contact and just say 'thank you' at the end of each explanation. The both of you then follow up by saying, 'I forgive myself', at the same time. There is truly no separation between the two of you.

The lists will reveal to you how you have judged others and yourself. What you see in others is really a reflection of that aspect in yourself; they are one and the same thing. The people who are in your life, mirror back an aspect of yourself. Relationships can only hold together whilst you are mirroring aspects to each other. When you can no longer see an aspect of yourself in another person then the field energy that existed between the two of you is severed and the relationship falls apart. When this happens it is evidence of someone's evolution.

It is not only all right but also righteous for you to have many close relationships. You are merely looking for someone who reflects what you are. It is evidence of your evolution; self is driven to find self, the perfect reflection. So it is that your total list and the emotions you experience represent those aspects of yourself that

Ride with the Wind

you need to deal with and master.

Now that you can make a start at dealing with your emotional body, let us take a brief look at the third row. The usherette shines her torch and at the same time tells you that few people are aware of what is really happening on the Power row.

Well, there they all are, all of those common faces and they are not occupying the most powerful seats! There is a hierarchy of power with 'King Rat' and 'King Lizard' sitting in the large chairs in the central aisle. The Politicians to your surprise, are sitting in the smaller chairs and she explains that they are really the middle management who are controlled from above and are simply mediators who convey messages to the people. Although they appear very relaxed they are really very compromised because of their lies. Two dark forces that have different agendas for mankind are controlling them.

Firstly, there are the financiers, a dozen powerful families of international bankers who are controlling the world's money supply. They are a group of tyrants who are achieving world domination by manipulating countries into indebtedness. The world is effectively bankrupt and they are just waiting for the right moment to pull the plug. Their net is widening and we see this with loans to countries from the International Monetary Fund and the World Bank. Here in Britain, who do you think is controlling the economy? The Bank of England, of course. And who owns the bank? Their net is also closing in on an individual level, again through the banking system. The European Monetary Union is another one of their control mechanisms. The World is gradually being merged into one fiscal platform...

You ponder this and ask, 'what is their motive and what are they waiting for?'

Our usher continues, 'they are power-crazy mercenaries and their god is Money. They understand about reincarnation and how they can choose their genetic line of rebirth. Their motive, therefore, is to be the controllers of this planet for generations to come, by keeping all of its peoples enslaved to them; thus protecting their future time-line positions. They cannot pull the plug to achieve global surrender until their banking technology is in place and they have removed cash from your societies or declared it worthless. The technology is already on trial and you can see this by the use of debit cards and smart cards with their computer chips. They have linked these to telecommunication companies and already most people and their lives are on their computers. They will soon introduce their smart cards to replace and streamline the normal banking functions but for the moment their computers are struggling to handle the volumes and they are experimenting with the security aspects under the guise of credit card fraud.

The second dark force is alien intervention on your planet. Most of you are

Ride with the Wind

unaware of this intervention or indeed of aliens themselves. You think that this speck of dust on the edge of the Milky Way is the only planet that harbours life! You even ignore the plethora of evidence confirming alien visitations dating back to before your Second World War. Your bookstores are full of this evidence.

When you consider that there are more than ten billion suns each with orbiting planets, supporting life, your mind needs to expand!

There are many types and races of aliens but in a greater understanding they are all your brothers and sisters. Just like you, they are consciousness and energy, spirit and soul, that has consummated itself into matter; matter itself being a manifestation of the thought that God is.

The different species differ only in their conscious evolvement and their genetic make-up, and therefore differ in their intelligence and the appearance of their bodies. I am only going to mention the ones that interact with this planet. All of them have influenced your genes over the centuries and your bodies are the result of twenty-two mutations. That is why you have so many different bodily characteristics and colours of skin. There are three main groups that are extraterrestrial. They are the Andromedans, the Pleiadians and the Draconians. And one group that is innerterrestrial!

The Andromedans are the Great Gods and will only intervene in your affairs to protect you from annihilating yourselves. They are what is called Christ consciousness and they sit on the seventh row. They can look down and see every seat in this cinema. They are fully-realised interdimensional entities. They include the likes of Yeshua, Ramtha and Buddha.

The Pleiadians are, in the main, benevolent beings, and follow a strict, non-interference code of conduct. They are also human-like in appearance and closely resemble you, especially if you are over seven feet tall! Their home is known as the Seven Sisters.

The Draconians consist of Reptilians and Greys and they believe they can mess with you as much as they want! They are merciless tyrants. The Reptilians look like a cross between a human being and an alligator and they are big and strong but slow. They are very psychic and can hypnotise you, just by looking at you.

The Greys are the most common type of alien encountered and are small humanoid entities with a bluish-grey coloured skin. They have large almond-shaped eyes, no ears and just a slit for a mouth. They do not eat, they live on prana, which means knowledge, and they communicate telepathically. They are also hypnotic but are subjugate to the Reptilians.

Ride with the Wind

A group of Pleiadian rebels have aligned themselves with the Draconians of the Orion constellation. Sometimes these types plus Praying Mantis type aliens, have been reported by abductees to be on the same craft at the same time. They have a common interest, which involves experimentation on humans.

It is these groups, from the Orion constellation, that you need to try and understand. Their forefathers lied to them, just as your forefathers have lied to you. Some of the Reptilians believe they are Royalty and that they are the rightful owners of this planet and you are their slaves. They seek to control and enslave you and they are winning the battle. For more details read the David Icke books.

The Reptilians now occupy positions of influence in your governments, your financial world, your military, intelligence and law enforcement agencies, and your religions. The few of them effectively control your world and should be thought of in terms of the agents in the film the Matrix.

The Greys are an old and dying race that had stopped breeding because they became devoid of emotion, as a result of making their god 'intellectual'. They literally bred in knowledge and bred out emotion. Because you have a wide range of strong emotions in your genetic make-up, they want your genes to breed back emotion; thereby saving themselves from extinction. Reports of abductions are true. They have been on your planet since the 1930's to steal your seed and eggs so that their siblings can experience emotion again.

After hearing all of this, you are stunned and need to sit down! You ask the usherette if you can join her on the fourth row and she says, 'you can sit there temporarily but if you want to take up your permanent seat you will need to move your energy permanently out of the first three rows'.

You ask her to explain this and she says, 'to free yourself from the first three rows you have to understand life to the point that you become completely objective about it. In other words, you have to centre yourself by taking a neutral, non-judgemental stance towards all life. That does not mean to say that you have to abstain from life and become a hermit. On the contrary, you can only understand life by living it. It is not so much the activities that you pursue as your conscious intent behind them. For instance, you can be a passionate person and love your partner unconditionally. You can occupy a position of power in your society but righteously exercise that power for the purposeful good of all.

When you come to understand and accept that you are indeed an immortal being, this automatically engenders a state of morality in you.

The thought of immortality in and of itself brings about this reality. In short, you

Ride with the Wind

will be living an impeccable lifestyle because you have mastered your emotional and mental bodies and your consciousness and energy is then permanently seated on the fourth row in unconditional love. There is no lack in love'.

Your curiosity gets the better of you and you wonder how one can possibly go beyond the fourth row. She picks up on your thoughts and says, 'as with all the rows, the fifth row is simply the next evolutionary step and the home of very advanced souls. These seats are occupied by entities who not only love unconditionally but who express their truth without duality or compromise. There is no room for emotion or hypocrisy here. The sixth row is a gateway to the seventh and represents your final initiate test. You will know what it is you need to conquer before you get there. The seventh row, of course, is God fully expressing through mankind. It is Godwoman or Godman, otherwise known as Christ consciousness. Very few of you have completed the journey home and yet there is no limitation on the number of seats available! Every one of you is worthy if you think you are, indeed, you are divine. It is *your* thoughts that count'.

You take her hand and she leads you to a temporary seat on the fourth row. Straight away you notice a different atmosphere in the cinema. You sit down and it is like being put in a bath of pure love, so you soak there whilst you view your old world. You begin to realise that it is all just one great big drama, a drama in which everybody is playing the role they want to, otherwise they wouldn't be doing it. You recognise that the wonderful creation of your body has deceived you, by masking the light of your true self, and that this plane of matter is the greatest illusion ever created by you and everyone else. You think, If only they could see what I am now seeing and know what I now know. You look upon your brothers and sisters with understanding and compassion and the love you feel overwhelms you.

You now understand that through your many lifetimes you have always been a 'somebody', a Phantom that has played many parts, only to become lost in the material illusions of life. Thus you separated yourself from God, the one and only true reality there is. You had become the single droplet of sea water, standing alone and weak in its power, not realising that when it is returned to the ocean; it has all the power of the ocean. The real power is with the imageless 'nobody'.

You are sitting on the fourth row, suspended in God's love, and you can now see that everything is immersed in this pure love. It is the cosmic glue that holds everything together, the very platform upon which you live. You now realise that your journey in life is to master your mortal thoughts and bring forth your spiritual body, your true self, the love of God from within you. The only way forward is atonement with this pure love. You have descended from Heaven and now you must ascend back to Heaven.

Ride with the Wind

As you sit and ponder this, you are given a vision of a New World, where the streets are literally paved in gold. There is a peace and harmony in this New World, which comes from the tranquillity of unconditional love. It is a pure and clean environment with unsurpassed beauty and you can see an interconnectedness between all life. It is a world that is free of drugs, crime and disease; and it has a mindset that is unified instead of being divided. Furthermore, there are no tyrants; there is no suppression of the people or propagation of disease. The people live as 'masters' in their immortal bodies. You realise that this is the home of those great souls who occupy permanent seats on the fifth row. Love conquers all is the thought that beholds you.

The movie suddenly comes to a close and you become a little confused. The usherette appears for the last time and you ask her, 'where am I and how can I keep in touch with you?' She replies, 'you are inside your own head, inside your subconscious mind. The movie screen is the frontal lobe of your brain and it's your thoughts, as light propellants, that are projecting onto the screen!'

She continues, 'I am you, you only need to go within yourself and ask what it is you desire; this is where all your answers have always been! Know that the moment you go within and ask a question or hold a picture of your desire, the manifestation of it is already in motion to you. At the same time give thanks to God, the source of the manifestation, and you shall receive your every wish; it is absolute universal law'.

Her parting words to you are, 'you should never struggle to be anything greater than what you already are because there is no such thing. When you realise that the struggle of life is really an illusion and that life is an all-allowing expression, then you are no longer a separate droplet of sea water but have become the almighty ocean; the power of pure love: once again atonement with God'.

Ride with the Wind

THE CHILDREN OF BLUE LIGHT

This story was inspired by Ramtha's teachings on the Void and the journey of Involution.

Once upon a time there was a Black Hole with nothing in it. Imagine it - just like the sky at night without any stars or a moon.

Then one day something happened. You see, the Black Hole can do something you can do. It can think and it decided it didn't just want to be a Black Hole anymore. And so it got all stirred up, just like a witch's cauldron, and it created something. What do you think it was?

It was a bright light! A brilliant blue shining light, brighter than any light you can remember. And it lit up the Black Hole. Now this blue light was no ordinary light, it was very special indeed. It could think like the Black Hole and it could move around like lightning because it had lots of energy - just like you!

And so for a very long time the blue light played and danced around in the Black Hole, flickering and shimmering its light everywhere it went. It was like a blue star that dances in the sky at night. Have you seen the blue star that dances in our sky or do the clouds cover it up at night like a big blanket? Go and look out of your bedroom window and see if you can spot it.

One day the blue light thought, 'I'm getting fed up with darting around this Black Hole, wherever I go I always seem to end up back at the same place; it's as if I've gone nowhere! Everywhere looks the same, nothing but velvet black space; beautiful but boring! And worse, I've got no one to play with and I don't know what I am!'

You see, it didn't know it was a Blue Star because it couldn't see itself. The Black Hole heard all of this and because it wanted to keep its only child happy, it got all stirred up again and guess what happened this time?

You guessed it! The Black Hole had some more children, little friends to play with its first child, the Blue Star. However, the Black Hole went a bit mad with its birthing process; it didn't limit itself to having just two or three sons and daughters: it created trillions of brothers and sisters for the first Blue Star to play with. They were all exactly the same, just like identical twin brothers and sisters. It was like looking in a hall of mirrors. And they could feel each other's energy and read each other's thoughts, because they all shared the same mind - the mind of the Black Hole.

Ride with the Wind

The first Blue Star had now become a Mother and a Father to a family of Sons and Daughters that were all made from the same blue light.

Well, can you imagine how the first Blue Star must have felt? One minute it was sad and all alone with no-one to play with, then the next minute it had trillions of friends and it could see its own reflection in all of them! 'I'm a Blue Star!' it said, 'and all of my Sons and Daughters are Blue Stars too'.

They all had trillions of playmates to play with and every time they looked upon each other, they understood that it was the same as looking in a mirror. They all played together, lighting up the Black Hole, and they loved each other beyond what words can express. How many friends do you have and do you love them all as if they were your brothers and sisters? Perhaps they really are...

Anyway, after many years had passed, a group of Blue Stars decided to go on an adventure, to see if they could find anything 'out there' in the Black Hole. This group were known as the 'brave ones'.

So off they wondered and the first Blue Star, who was their Mother/Father, stayed at home. Every so often the brave ones would come back home to tell about what they had experienced and their Mother/Father was always pleased to see them.

After a while a strange thing began to happen. The further they moved away from the first Blue Star, the darkness started to change colour and they started to slow down. It was as if light had come out of the darkness...

They were moving through some kind of gigantic rainbow and that's not all that happened. The gigantic rainbow was a Magic Rainbow; everytime they thought about something it just appeared in the colour of the atmosphere they were in. They got everything they could possibly dream of and in the twinkling of an eye!

They created different coloured suns that birthed orbiting planets. The heat from the suns, radiating upon the planets, created clouds that produced rains; which made the planets fertile for nurturing life. They also created homes for themselves, animals to play with, birds, trees, flowers, insects and vegetation: indeed, absolutely everything they could conjure up in their thoughts just appeared before them in the colour of the rainbow. Can you imagine the fun they were having?

As they moved through the colours of the Magic Rainbow, some of the Blue Stars started to get concerned because their blue lights were getting dimmer and dimmer, the further they moved away from the first Blue Star. They halted and thought, 'what if we were to disappear altogether?'

Ride with the Wind

Well, obviously no-one knew the answer to this question because they had never been this far from home before. They all became a little confused about knowing what to do.

They had come as far as the violet blue colour in the Magic Rainbow and they had created some beautiful things in this colour (and some ugly things too!). They had to make a decision - do they stay and live in this beautiful blue world or go back to the golden world that they created just prior to arriving in the blue? Or do they carry on with their adventure into the colours of the Magic Rainbow?

Some of them decided to go all the way back to their Mother/Father to tell of their experiences, and in doing so, their blue lights became as bright as ever. Others decided to stay in the Golden and Blue worlds because it was so beautiful there. We now know them as Angels. The really brave ones decided to say goodbye to their brothers and sisters and carry on with their journey into the unknown. What do you think they found?

Well, eventually they came to a bridge that was like a massive blue spider's web and its lace shimmered in the blue sunset. When they looked through the fine web of the bridge, a long way down they could see a new world. It was our world and it looked wonderful to them. They then realised that some of their brothers and sisters had passed this way before them and had beaten them to the bridge; they had created this beautiful planet that looked like an Emerald Jewel and had jumped from the bridge!

The Blue Stars couldn't wait to get here! So they jumped from the spider-webbed bridge into the darkness of night and they fell for what seemed to be endless miles.

A weird thing happened as they fell through the night sky. They were now slowing down more and more and the sky was becoming thick and foggy. They fell into a long, deep sleep, even though they had never experienced being asleep before! They were being scattered all over this world and when they finally woke up, they found themselves inside little bodies. What they didn't know was that half of them had become baby girls and the other half had become baby boys...

They were now baby girls and boys that had forgotten that they were really Blue Stars, because their new bodies were covering up their brilliant, blue light, and they had somehow lost their memories in the fall from the blue spider-webbed bridge. They couldn't even remember jumping off the bridge!

What do you think could have caused them to lose their memories? Perhaps their memories were not really lost but remained hidden somewhere inside of them.

Ride with the Wind

When they finally woke up, the daylight was shining in their faces and they could feel and hear things moving around them. This was an unusual playground. 'Where am I and what am I?', they thought to themselves.

Fortunately, as they grew up, some of the Blue Stars started to remember bits and pieces of their past journey and began to realise that they were more than just a human body. They became aware that they had some form of magic power inside of themselves, because some of them began to be able to move objects simply by using the power of their minds. They felt like they had some kind of Sleeping Giant inside of them that was waking up from a long, deep sleep. How could they fully wake up the Sleeping Giant and get their power back?

They had to understand that their power had never gone away in the first place. It had always been there just like the way embers burn from a great fire. Their power had simply become run down but could be rekindled at any time. What they needed to learn, to wake up the unseen Giant, was to love themselves in exactly the same way as they had loved each other when they were Blue Stars.

Love was the answer to getting their power back.

Sadly, some of the Blue Stars never got to wake up the Sleeping Giant. They looked into the mirrors of this world and reasoned that they were nothing more than their reflection. It is understandable for them to think that way but what if they knew the truth - that they had lost their hidden power to an illusion! Never did they ask the question, 'what's this awesome power that sits behind my eyes?'

They lived their illusionary lives as if they were nothing more than a human body and consequently they eventually died and thus never made it back to their real home above the blue spider-webbed bridge.

Only a handful of them worked it all out for themselves. They were the emerging geniuses. They realised that they were just *passing through* this world to experience all they desire from it, and then to take that wisdom back home to the first Blue Star; the one they regarded as their real Mother and Father. Only when they had realised every facet of this illusionary life, did they get the power from the Giant within.

The power descended upon them like a flock of doves. The Giant in them was now fully awake and its power issued forth in their lives. Although they were still living in this slow world, they could now create anything they wanted and as quickly as if they were still living in the Blue or Golden worlds. Because they were now shining like diamonds, they were known as the 'Shining Ones'.

Ride with the Wind

Eventually, the Shining Ones had experienced everything they wanted from this world and they realised it was time for a new adventure. They became so powerful that the mere thought of returning to the blue spider-webbed bridge, lifted them up to it. From there they would plan their next adventure.

Some of them went on to experience life on other planets and they found that when they descended to those planets, they were always clothed in a suitable body for the different environments they encountered.

The rest of them went all the way home to the first Blue Star, who had built a fabulous home for them. It was bathed in a beautiful golden light and there played a symphony of the most wonderful music, which seemed to come from the light itself. It was and is known as The City of Light.

The table was set for their homecoming. It was to be a Royal Banquet. All of the names of the Shining Ones were already printed on the chairs that awaited their Royal presence. They ate and drank like the fully-realised gods they had become.

And so the Sons and Daughters of the first Blue Star are spread high and low and far away. There are the two dimensional 'Flatlanders' who never moved far from home. There are the 'Angelic Ones' who have always lived in the Blue and Golden worlds. There are the 'Trapped Ones' who have got trapped by their own illusions upon a world like this. There are the 'Intergalactic Travellers' who have learned how to time-travel and finally there are the 'Royal Shining Ones' who have done it all.

If you were a Blue Star which group would you be in? Perhaps you really are a Blue Star but think you are what you see in the mirror? You can change group at any time if you can learn to see beyond your own illusions! Sweet dreams my precious Blue Star.

Ride with the Wind

WHAT IS REALITY?

Science has now brought us all to the point where we should be asking the question - what is reality?

A good example to illustrate this, is to ask whether the brain can distinguish between sex and masturbation? If people were really honest, they'd have to admit that there have been times when they've had sex with a person and they've had their eyes closed; or it's been pitch black or they've been the worse for alcohol or drugs. So what process has been occurring to achieve the desired result? And is it really any different if they are self-stimulating or with a partner?

Staying with the same theme, we recognise that it is either our environment that is stimulating us, or it is our past memories or our fantasies; and more often than not, it is a combination of all three things! Our bodies simply don't care how the emotional release through orgasm comes about; just that it happens when the chemical build-up becomes too great. And it's exactly the same process with greed, victimisation, tyranny, pain, suffering; indeed, every emotional addiction produces these body chemicals that crave satisfaction (redemption) e.g. anger, overeating, bullying, shyness ectcetera.

When we set aside looks and body parts, we see that people only really differ by the attitudes they are displaying, which are coming from the neurological hard-wiring that has occurred because of past, mind-associated, environmental memories. Once a person has experienced most things, the environment generally offers nothing new, but just stimulates this past associated memory. And as the brain cannot distinguish between what it is looking at and its memory, then our realities are most certainly based in the past, because they are coming off of thinking that is nothing more than environmentally triggered memories!

So let's answer the question. Reality is occurring moment by moment and it plays out in accordance with the moment by moment firing of holographic images in the brain, regardless of whether the images are occurring with our eyes open or with them closed. When we add to this - that 'thinking is the firing of holographic images onto the frontal lobe of the brain' - we have to conclude that reality is simply what we think it to be!

Reality, just like truth, is subjective. Even the most objective mind only ever expresses personal truth.

This begs another question - how do we change our personal reality? It's probably best to answer this with a another question - if you are getting all worked up about something in your life and you're heading towards an emotional climax, how can

Ride with the Wind

you change the outcome of that event? You simply have to put the brakes on that train of thought (a neurologically hard-wired attitude), stop it dead in its tracks and continue with a different train of thought that has a more desirous outcome.

Have you ever thrown somebody's thinking onto another subject when they were obviously steeped in an attitude that was causing them some anguish? Well, self-mastery is all about becoming so conscious that you effectively do exactly that to yourself, all of the time; and thus finally create a reality that is not a reflection of your past but is what you want to become free of it.

Imagine for a moment that you're being a quiet observer, on a train platform, watching the 'trains of thought' come and go. Then you get on one of the trains and those harmful neuro-peptides start to flow in your body; blocking cellular receptor sites that would otherwise be used for nutritional uptake. Do you get off at the next stop and return to being the 'observer' on the platform before it's too late? Or do you continue journeying with the train of thought until it reaches its climactic destination?

Most people are so unconscious that they don't even realise they are on a train, with generally only one opportunity to get off it before they feel their addiction to a journey they've done so many times before.

The master is the one that is always left on the platform after the train has left, and if they inadvertently get caught up in the crowd and find themselves on a train; they always get off at the next stop.

Perhaps this is the reason why 'masters of old' used to retreat from society for a period of time (like 40 days and nights), so as to purge their demons and purify their thoughts, to achieve a greater personal reality.

If you observe your mind, you'll notice that unmarked trains are passing moment by moment. You don't need to concern yourself with these because they are just the result of the platform you are standing upon. However, if you take a fancy to one of these and you ride it for a while, then you'll only be able to stop it dead in it's tracks if you name it (spite, envy etc.). So, if you're really smart, that's exactly what you'll do, because otherwise you've got another runaway train that's going to a destination that you've frequented so many times before.

Don't be disheartened if you are unable to name all of your trains at first because you need a lot of experience before you know the outcome of events beforehand; and thus become a master trainspotter! And then you will wait patiently, observing all the trains going to the boring destinations, until the train you really want comes flying in - Destination Freedom - climb on board!

Ride with the Wind

What now follows is an example relating to a question I had from a woman I had counselled. She had a pattern of falling prey to one man after another and as she consciously took her power back she swung to find she then had control issues.

Question (from her) - in order for my life to change didn't I need to gain control?

Great question that's also logical but control is just another emotion! It certainly 'feels' much better to be in control than to be sexual prey doesn't it? Do you see what I mean?

In terms of the train analogy - you've simply re-named your train and thus changed its chemical destination to the climax you 'feel' when you demonstrate that you are in control. But where is the master? She is still on the platform because she recognised both of the trains and named those 'trains with attitudes' as they passed by. You only named the one train (victim) and thus when you got off it, you immediately boarded the train going in the opposite direction (tyrant); and once again you passed the master waving at you from the platform!

Now here's what you need to understand - the master is you, but to become what you really are; you have to stand in her shoes by staying on the platform seemingly out of control. You see, when you're 'in control' it feels good but the bottom line is - you're just giving your body another chemical hit that's causing you to age and eventually to die - whereas, the master is eternally young because she rarely boards the chemical trains and if she does, she gets off before it's too late. I hope I have explained this clearly enough.

We never want to arrive at the already known destination of one of these attitudes, unless we're happy to keep marching towards our own death. Indeed, ageing only occurs by boarding 'trains with attitudes' that are ironically 'out of control' and always have the same kind of destination - emotional reaction.

You need to recognise all of your feelings in order to be able to name all of your 'trains of thought', to be able to stay on the platform. In other words, your every conscious moment from now on should be consumed with trainspotting until you are like the master that just smiles as the trains pass by.

Why do you think people turn up in your life that you don't particularly want to see? It's because you've boarded a train that you previously boarded with them! And behold they're still on the train and walk through from the next carriage! If you'd have got off at the first stop and returned to the platform, you'd never have seen them again.

They were still journeying on the same train because they are still a sexual

Ride with the Wind

predator, and they constantly meet sexual prey (victims) on that train. However, they also have less than a comfortable journey when they sit next to someone who is riding with a controlling attitude. They feed off of the energy from their victims but they starve in anger when somebody else is in control.

Your pendulum may have swung away from victimisation, but if you're still 'courting the chemical addiction' then it will swing to the other side and take on a new name. So, in this instance (and there are many examples), on the one track we have the train with the victim attitude and on the other track we have the train with the tyrannical attitude. Both trains have a chemical destination that is detrimental to the health of your body. And on the platform we still have the master recognising all of the trains. The master's is where the pendulum sits still.

Finally, when we have identified ALL of the trains on this platform then the game is over - we have become the master of this environment. It's time for a new game! There is nothing new for us to learn here, so it's time for us to contemplate upon that which we have yet to realise - a new platform.

We know that this world is comprised of atoms and that the next world is comprised of sub-atomic particles, which are at least a billion times smaller than the atoms. We also know that if we shrunk everything down in size in this world, then it would look the same as it does now. So the relative size of the next platform to this platform is irrelevant, once you're participating on it... But how do we get there without any point of reference? We can only contemplate upon it and desire to know it. And once we are truly free of the passing trains of this world, then the new platform will appear to us and we will be lifted to it.

Your thinking affects the chemistry in your body and this in turn, causes cellular ageing or rejuvenation; dependent only upon whether you continue to journey in your mind to known destinations or you join the masters who are contemplating upon new adventures.

Part 2

The Blue Window

INTRODUCTION

I don't know anybody who is like I am, who thinks the way I think, who knows what I know and who sees what I see. I am an individual. And so are you! I suppose you could call me a visionary because I have a vision of a brave new world, where the problems we have today, simply don't exist.

I am not wishing to make this sound too simplistic, but all of the problems we have are a reflection of our attitudes and the collective consciousness that prevails here. The only way we are going to overcome the issues that haunt us and move towards improving our society, is to revolutionise the way that we all think. Collectively, we must now move away from the sexual revolution and our warring natures and all the unpleasantness that that has brought; and move towards a divine revolution that will heal us as a truly international community. Individually, we must change our attitudes and our minds. Only then will we eventually live in harmony with one another.

Can you imagine helping to create a beautiful future for yourself and your family, where everyone respects nature and the free will of every individual? This can become a reality but only if we all make a decision to change, to grow and to evolve beyond everything we have hitherto known.

Today, the governments of the world have some very clever psychics working for them. According to Ramtha the Philadelphia experiment was a true happening. Their psychics have literally ripped time! They have time-travelled to our future and seen a beautiful future for all of humanity. From their perspective, there's only one problem with it - it doesn't include them wielding power over us. Neither does it include the powerful religions of the world. There is no room for tyranny and 'control freaks' in the future days on earth. The power of love will reign supreme and that is something that can't be harnessed or controlled. The age of God is upon us and this has nothing to do with religion.

Our spiritual destiny is to live in a world that is full of truthful beings, who have freedom of expression and who respect the free will of everyone. This is a world that lives in harmony by virtue of its super-consciousness. It is a moralistic world that requires few rules and regulations, just a 'peoples charter' that everyone values and upholds. This new order is a world without tyranny and mind control. It is therefore a world without the kind of governmental rule and religious authority

The Blue Window

we are mind-controlled by today. Out of chaos will eventually come order. The beautiful butterfly will eventually emerge from the chrysalis of the caterpillar.

If this sounds too idealistic then please consider the following. The reason we have the problems we have is due to us not having a lofty ideal that we can collectively work towards of our own free will. Just take a look at the ideals that our children have. The world's media heavily influences them. The governments control their school curriculum and their medication. The religions brainwash them. There is a lack of quality parenting. And peer pressure still exerts the most dominant influence. The result is our children have no cohesive direction to work towards a better future and many are getting health problems as a result of being slowly poisoned.

It's September 2000 and in Northern Ireland we have little children being ferried to school behind armed guards, dodging bombs being hurled at them, and obviously frightened out of their wits! What kind of childhood memories are they going to have? And what is the cause of this obvious divide in consciousness? RELIGION. We can't continue to live off a 2000 year-old memory of a magnificent being who gave us an ideal to follow but whom instead we have abused as an idol and worshipped in a vein to satisfy our own needs and greed.

What do you think Jesus thinks about the Protestant and Catholic religions? I can tell you - he abhors them! In fact, he is fervently against all religion because it only serves to enslave the minds of mankind. He loves the individual worshipper and recognises their ignorance in worshipping him but he is against any so-called authority that stands in between God and Mankind; professing to have the sole word of God and to be the only route to God. To anyone with a modicum of intelligence, this is clearly not the case.

When are we all going to wake up and realise that we've all been given the free will to create whatever reality we want and whatsoever we choose to create; we only have to take responsibility for it.

Far from loving free will we seem to be a species that positively leaps to surrender it, whenever we can! - Matt Ridley, author of GENOME

You only get to live in this 'brave new world' by engaging the knowledge in this book and allowing it to sit with your truth. Knowledge is the key that opens the door to understanding. There is not a problem with having a One World Order. It is only a problem when it is driven by a tyrannical consciousness, because then it violates an individual's free will to choose without influence, persuasion, bribary, manipulation, threat or demand.

The Blue Window
MIND CONTROL

There is a science known as Quantum Mechanics or Quantum Physics, which few people are aware of and even fewer have studied. And yet this science has been with us for over 100 years! Why has it not been taught in our schools? The governments and Christian religions of the world have kept its knowledge from us. Why? Because it works, it is a higher truth and it empowers the individual; exactly what those who control us don't want - a society of freethinking, powerful individuals. Sheep are easy to control but free-flying eagles are not.

Quantum Mechanics has demonstrated that it is the 'observer' that creates reality. And who is the observer? You and I that's who! This is scientific fact. Our collective reality is actually a collection of each individual's created reality. And an individual's created reality is being created, most often unconsciously, by every thought that that individual has. That's what the authorities don't want you to know. It empowers you when you realise you can create any reality you want by changing the way you think and you're not really a victim of external influences, unless you think you are.

Our minds affect the particle behaviour of the subatomic world and it is the subatomic world that underpins everything that we see. So we get to see what we expect to see. Why do you think humanity evolves very slowly and thus our world changes very slowly? It's because we are constantly reaffirming an old reality; we recreate the environment and conditions in our bodies everyday by thinking how we did yesterday...

We think the here and now is what we are looking at, but in fact, Quantum Mechanics tells us that what we are looking at, is in actual fact, the past. We keep reaffirming the past into the future. The now is what we focus upon in our minds, not the environment we look upon or the body we wear. We entangle this creative now moment in what we look upon instead of intentionally creating reality through our minds.

Let me try and give you a simple example. I worked as an holistic therapist, performing a variety of alternative and complementary therapies; to help my patients overcome their physical and emotional problems. With most patients, I explained to them that their mind and their body are not separate. I told them that they can discern the two but the two are not really separate. This is not mumbo jumbo; again it is scientific fact. And the jam in the sandwich is the emotional body. Here's how it works:

The conclusion of your thought processes, after analysis, is communicated to your body in two ways, chemically and electrically. Your endocrine system

The Blue Window

comprises a number of ductless glands, which secrete chemicals called neuro-peptides and various hormones. These are chemical messengers that travel through your brain and your blood stream, carrying information to the cells and organs of your body. Your nervous system, similarly, communicates information, but does it electrically, down your nerves down to your big toes! Nerve impulses are electrical messengers. Your body is therefore affected by the way you think. Your thought is the *cause*; your body is the *effect*. As the effect follows the cause, your body therefore conforms to your past thinking. When you look at your body in the mirror you are looking at the past! So if you look at yourself and think 'you big fat ---' then you always will be!

To prove my point, I had eczema on my left foot for a few months. At the time of writing, it came about 3 years ago and I tried every lotion and potion going, to try and rid myself of it. Recently afterwards, it just disappeared! I can only put it down to one thing. In the months that proceeded, I was too busy to think about it and even forgot to apply any cremes. It was my mind that was holding the condition in place by my focusing upon it. Although the original cause was stress-related, it was my mind that kept reaffirming the condition into the future, way beyond my stressful period. **What we focus upon in our lives, we empower**. Take your mind off it for a lengthy period and it will go away.

Similarly, what we think about our environment determines how we treat it and obviously this is the platform upon which we live. It conforms to the collective consciousness of all us viewers 'observing' it. If we want to live in a clean environment then it can only be achieved by standing up for change. When we individually change we will change the collective consciousness and the environment will eventually heal itself, just like night follows day.

The governments and Christian religions are well acquainted with the science of Quantum Mechanics. They know that the collective mindset is what is creating the conditions here. And they like the current conditions because it keeps them in control and this serves their lust for power and greed. It should now be obvious that for the tyrants to stay in control, all they have to do is keep the people thinking the way they've always thought! Mind control the population and you will always control the world. Keep people's focus on their bodies, how they look and their emotions, how they feel; and you easily control them.

All the 'graymen' have to do to completely control the people is control the food supply (they already control the money supply). Are you starting to get the picture?

Mind control is not a new concept. It has been going on for centuries. It is the authorities best kept secret, until now. It is pervasive in our society. Just look at

The Blue Window

the trash that comes through the media and where the focus is. Sex, drugs, gossip, fashion, competitive sport, violence, wars, need I go on? All they have to do is keep us focused on this stuff. We can't watch Big Brother or Eastenders every week without it affecting the way we think, which stimulates our emotional addictions, and this is creating our reality; the kind of reality the 'graymen' want us to have because it keeps them in control.

Business media marketing is all about mind control, the use of subliminal programming - see if you can spot it in their advertising.

Do you know how effective their mind control programmes are? So effective that you don't know and you think they don't exist! Do not underestimate the power of mind control but do become more aware of it. To heal our living conditions we must first reveal the causes of our disharmony.

The media is obviously one of the weapons of mind control. It's not just what is said but also the frequencies at which it is being delivered. The more you switch off and live in your world, the more of a freethinking individual you will become. Or are you too addicted emotionally? Have a real good think about that one...

I listened to some personal development tapes by a psychological trainer. I am in agreement with Brian Tracey when he says 'there are two forces in the world today, the one is the power of love, the other is the power of suggestion'. If you don't want to live in a better world then continue to subject yourself to the power of suggestion. Indeed, just continue to be like you've always been! If, on the other hand, you are fed up with looking at and listening to the same old stuff, then stop looking at it and listening to it, and get a new vision. Ignore what's going on around you and just be concerned about where your focus is. Your personal reality will always reflect where your focus is, at any given time.

As Brian Tracey says 'leaders are readers - the top 1% of our society are people who read at least 12 non-fiction books a year. That's an average of 1 a month. And most of them also listen to audio tapes on self-development and go to educational seminars'. Unfortunately, the other 99% would rather go to the pub, go to the gym, go to the cinema, watch soapy dramas, watch or play competitive sport, go on holidays, have sex or look at stimulating pictures, and read about the relationships of the rich and famous! Have I missed anything?

What staggers me is that we've got all the information about mind control staring us in the face and yet we are either too blind to see it, too scared to do anything about it or too happy being controlled. We even make films such as 'Conspiracy Theory' and we see them as good, wacky, far-fetched entertainment! I'm sure most of the general public believe these films to be not real life depictions, and believe

The Blue Window

the conspiracy investigators to be mislead, paranoid, outcasts of society.

The 'powers that be' know that a minority of outrageously sane individuals cannot affect the collective consciousness of the masses whilst the masses are focused on their emotions. So they allow us to continue unhindered, not wishing to corroborate the evidence by doing something stupid like killing us; but far better to pull on the emotional strings of the masses by mocking us.

Is it really too hard for you to believe that there are mind-controlled assassins who have been programmed by the employees of the western government's intelligence agencies, using techniques similar to those portrayed in the movie 'Conspiracy Theory'? And is it too hard for you to swallow that there are many 'Alice in Wonderland' sexual slaves that do plenty of programmed swallowing to satisfy the grotesque sexual desires of some of our world's leading public personalities? If you would like to know more about mind control and the secret lives of some of our world's leading public personalities then may I suggest you start by reading Trance Formation of America by Philips and O'Brien.

The Blue Window

FREE WILL

In Matt Ridley's book GENOME, he writes, 'the modern Christian consensus is that God has implanted free will in us, so that we have a choice of living virtuously or in sin'. That being the case, then why do the Christian religions violate our free will by trying to influence our choices with the imposition of their will? Power, control, money, greed, self-interest, I hear it all. From the same book, 'everybody's fate is determined not by their genes but by their controlled environment' and 'Rich Harris lays bare just how much more alarming social determinism is than genetic. It is brainwashing. Far from leaving room for free will it rather diminishes it'. And 'It is odd that so many writers who defend human dignity against the tyranny of our genes seem happy to accept the tyranny of our surroundings'. Thanks for that Matt!

Free will is our God-given right to express ourselves, however we choose, but obviously within the laws of the land we *chose* to live in. When there is no longer a choice, the game is up; we have a collapsed consciousness. We are rapidly moving towards this point, under the current tyrannical leadership. I want to make my position clear here. I am against any act that violates an individual's free will of expression. Some obvious acts that spring to mind are murder, rape, blackmail, kidnapping, terrorism, threats and mind control. Mind control is by far the greatest violation of free will. And the two biggest perpetrators are the world's religions and governments. If there is such a thing as sin then this is it because it violates our God-given right to express freely our creative will.

To my mind, tyranny is sinful and mind control is the main weapon of the tyrants. But is it wrong? No! To judge the tyrant as being wrong would be a limited truth that would keep us being victims to them. We must try to understand that all of us have at times in our lives been tyrannical, by trying to impose our will on someone else, to fulfill our need to be in control. These are simply experiences that we should all now be waking up from, by learning to love ourselves and everyone else - unconditionally.

Tyranny has many guises and it can be very subtle. For instance, thinking you are responsible for another adult is a subtle form of tyranny. It is just another self-created reality that some people have got consumed by and stuck in. What continues the reality is the sheep that play victim. Tyrants cannot exist without their followers...

Why do you think Tony Blair was urging people out to vote in the recent British elections? It was because he believes his power lies in being in control and so without a following he would be powerless. In his book The Seat of the Soul, Gary Zukav states clearly that this kind of power is both external and illusionary.

The Blue Window

The British elections were a good example of mind control. Labour got in because their propaganda machine was greater than the other two. And yet they only got 25% of the potential votes! And how many of these votes did they get because there was no credible alternative amongst the main players and seemingly no point in voting for a smaller party because they'd got no chance of getting in? On television, I only heard party political broadcasts from the three main players. What about proportional representation for the Green party and the other smaller parties! We will not have a fair system until they are all given the same amount to spend and an equal amount of airtime. The recent channel 4 programme, Politics isn't working, is a true statement. It was the smallest turnout since 1918.

The days of the tyrants are numbered. Without our support they are powerless. There is no need to riot, just withdraw your support. The people are fed up with control freaks who are full of their own self-interest and who take the piss by giving themselves 47k a year pay rises. And I am fed up with their lies, aren't you? Do you know any politician who tells the truth consistently 100% of the time? What kind of example are they setting the general public? No wonder the world is in such a mess!

The Blue Window

TRUTH

There is truth in everything. Every experience you have in life will hold an element of truth for you. And it's yours for the taking. Yet two people who have the same experience will probably walk away with different truths because of their differing prior experiences in life. And everybody's life is different, so therefore everybody's truth is different. Truth is a subjective reality; it is a personal thing. In other words, an individual's truth is the conclusion of an individual's cumulative experiences. We collect and compile truth in our lives from our experiences in the controlled environment that we live in. When we express an opinion that is not based upon our experience, then this is generally conjecture or somebody else's truth. We just show our ignorance when we do this.

Some people will really struggle with the above because they have been programmed to believe that there is an absolute truth, which is normally the truth of a religious way of thinking. Or they think there is but one truth - theirs! Are they wrong in their truth? Of course not - it is their truth. I hope you understand what I am saying here.

If I said to you that the one and only truth is, 'everything is God, including you and I', you would probably struggle to accept this because it is not your truth.

I have found that every school of knowledge has it's own truth. For us to consider it to be the one and only or absolute truth, would make our truth a very limiting one. I have also found there is truth in everything and there is always a higher order of that truth, until we finally reach our finest moment of realisation. And even then it is our realisation, indeed, it is our truth.

People who try to impose their truth on others are tyrants and their followers are victims. I accept that your truth will differ from mine and I am of the mind to allow you your truth. That is my level of understanding. That is an example of my love for you. Even if I recognise that somebody has a limited, ignorant truth; for me to try and force my truth down their throat, would make me a tyrant. And that is not what I am. Am I forcing you to read this book?

One can only recognise a lower truth when one has moved beyond it. To try and move somebody from that lower place, when they obviously need to experience it for their understanding, is a foolish thing to do. To do so only shows a lack of understanding of what truth is and how we grow through our own experiences.

There is another important ingredient that determines our ability to gain understanding and to move to the highest echelons of truth. It is philosophy of the highest order. Experience that is not coupled with lofty philosophy, will often

The Blue Window

be barren where truth is concerned or only yield a very basic understanding. Likewise, a philosophy, if it is not lived, will only ever remain a dry philosophy. So to become wise I have found that we have to acquire the lofty philosophy and then incorporate it into our lives through our own experiences.

I know of many people who are rich in experience but who lack in wisdom because they have never opened themselves up to the *deeper* knowledge. And I know of many others who have been given the loftiest of philosophies yet they fear to engage the new experiences necessary to move to a higher order of truth. They are great at regurgitating the philosophy but they will only get to own it as truth when they move beyond their comfort zones to experience it. Equally, this applies to me - I am here to know every word I have written, as my truth.

'And yet if we only knew how each loss of one's viewpoint is a progress and how life changes when one passes from the stage of the closed truth to the stage of the open truth - a truth like life itself, too great to be trapped by points of view, because it embraces every point of view...a truth great enough to deny itself and pass endlessly into a higher truth' - from Paths Beyond Ego - The Transpersonal Vision by Walsh and Vaughan.

If you would like to know more on this subject then there are some great DVD's entitled Revealing Truth to the Hidden Self, available from www.ramtha.com.

The Blue Window

PERFECTION

Perfection is a limitation of mind and an enslavement of oneself because it is a state of being that one can never attain; yet many strive for it. If there were a state of perfection then what would happen when you reached it? Where would you go from there? In terms of evolution, nothing can stand still, and if it does it dies. A state of perfection would mean the death of everything because in perfection there is no room for evolution. And all life evolves no matter how slowly.

The word evolution means change. So to evolve means to change. To change something that was considered perfect would make it imperfect. To not change from a hypothetical state of perfection would result in no evolution, no growth and no expansion. And that's not how it is. Everything is evolving albeit slowly in the case of humanity.

When we refuse to change we stop evolving. It's then a case of just 'treading water' and 'sucking air' until the day we die.

God is constantly growing, evolving and expanding itself. You've only got to look at nature to see that as a truth. The mind of God is constantly expanding through the contemplation of itself and the experiences of all of us, as participants and observers. If God ever reached a state of perfection, everything would cease to exist because there would be no evolution, only death.

Bearing this in mind, how can you now possibly think of God as being perfect? God is imperfect because God is forever changing, growing and expanding itself. You are not separate from God and never have been. It is only the way you have been taught to think that has created a separation in your mind. What if you could know what the mind of God knows? Well you can because the mind of God is your own subconscious mind, sitting in the lower cerebellum of your brain and everybody's brain! So you are here to make known the unknown, which is the same as saying to make conscious your subconscious mind.

Our evolutionary journey is therefore a *conscious* journey. Ask yourself this, if God is not perfect which God isn't, then why am I trying to be perfect and further why am I trying to impose my limitation of perfection onto others?

The perfectionists are their own worst enemies. They're striving for a concept that is a limitation of mind. It does not open and expand the mind; it contracts and closes it. They are tyrants because trying to impose a condition of perfection on self or upon others is a disallowing, unloving state of mind. Ironically, perfectionists become the victims of their own tyrannical thinking! But then, maybe, this serves them well? Time for another rethink?

The Blue Window

IDENTITY ENTRAPMENT

I am this, I am that, I am this way; I am that way: oh really? What if you are really none of the identities you so readily label yourself with and then hold onto with a vice grip?

Probably our biggest enslavement is the common identity of saying 'I am only human'. During the course of my therapy work, I helped to bridge many people from their self-imposed mental prisons to deeper levels of mind and I lost count of the amount of people who excused their behaviour by saying 'I'm only human'.

Are we human beings who are trying to be spiritual people or are we really spiritual beings who are having a human experience?

Imagine if you will. A teardrop of powerful energy, conscious, aware, unlimited, pure, divine, outrageous, bizarre, loving, giving, allowing, wilful, all knowing. That is what you really are. Now cloak it with a genetic garment of limitation (your body), which hides your true self and causes you to think that you are the garment. Now you have the illusion of the human condition. You think you are your body but you are really the intelligence that observes it from behind your eyes and from all around you. You are awesome and you don't even know it...

That which we are, consciousness and energy, spirit and soul; is the will that empowers us to be whatever we choose to be. Therefore, if we think we are our humanity then that's all we're ever going to be! But clearly there are two paths that we can take and *be* in our lives. We can be the Son or Daughter of Mankind and only ever know our humanity or we can rise above the human condition and be the Daughter or Son of God, the higher and greater understanding.

If you want to live the rest of your short life, living an illusion, then that is up to you. What you really are, your will, will empower you to be whatever you want to be. It is your wilfull desire that sets the wheels of manifestation into motion. Please do not excuse your behaviour on being human because it is your behaviour that determines whether you are human or not, and not the other way around.

What if you change your mind and decide to enact the highest principle in you instead of the lower? Are you then a human being? No, you become a god being. You become alienated to your humanity as you progressively disassociate with the lower principle in you. Is a Christ an alien? Absolutely! Christ consciousness is alien to human consciousness; it is the full expression of the highest principle in you and can only be fully realised whilst you're in a flesh and blood body. It is God fully realised in a man or in a woman. Godman / Godwoman = a Christ.

The Blue Window

So what am I? I am the observer who observes it all and who recognises that I am merely passing through this dimension, experiencing all of it and collecting pearls of wisdom for my soul. I am Spirit and Soul journeying in this dimension of consciousness, making known the unknown; indeed, making conscious the subconscious mind of God, in me.

How can I know truth unless I experience it for myself? I simply can't know truth without going into the marketplace of life, the great teacher, and observing it closely. I am here to experience the loftiest philosophy; not merely to play lip service to it, like an unenlightened philosopher.

It's not that we have to do everything in life or that we have to experience three dozen different occupations like I have done, no; this is not what I am saying here. What I am saying is that each time we forge an illusionary identity for our self, we put our self in a box, a comfort zone; and this limits our truth and thus it limits our reality.

What identities are you holding onto that are stopping you from moving forward in your acquisition of truth and wisdom?

In my life, I have come across a lot of women who have labelled themselves with a strong family identity. They are somebody's daughter, somebody's mother and somebody's wife. And they will fight to hold onto their self-created image. Add to this their occupation, if they have one, their house, their car and maybe the odd trip to the gym or coffee morning with friends: and you've almost got the complete identity. The trouble is, it's a complete fabrication! Is it also real? Yes! But only because you have limited your reality to what you are experiencing through the senses of your body. In truth you are not really a woman and I am not really a man - we are neither and both!

I said to a friend as we sat in a restaurant, I asked her, 'what would be the greatest illusion?' And she couldn't answer me. I said to her, 'would it not be the one that you are not aware of?' She agreed. I then said to her, 'take a look at all the people in this restaurant. They are all actors and actresses in the greatest drama there is; it's called life. Isn't this just the greatest illusion there is?'

One of the problems we have with experiences is knowing when they are over, because it is we who hold onto their identity. For instance, you can spend a lifetime pursuing a career, creating illusionary new barriers for you to overcome in your pursuit of perfection; yet it is only when you look objectively at the experience, do you realise that the wisdom has already been had and you're just holding on to the identity. Then you know it's time to throw the badge away and move on...

The Blue Window

Your intellectual mind will always move to justify you staying in an experience because it is the mind of compromise. And probably the biggest compromise is money. People get emotional about money; and it is the emotion that keeps them chained to the yoke. If you compromise your life for money or you make money your god then you'll only ever know a limited truth. There is nothing wrong in having money but there is a vast difference between living for truth and living for money. Living for truth means living and speaking your truth without duality or compromise.

Wisdom is not conditional upon your financial status in life. The state of your bank balance does not determine how wise you are. The problem I find with some wealthy people is the image that tends to go with them. They often become full of their own self-importance and display arrogant attitudes. This can also be said of some people without money who try to keep up with the Jones's and think they're better than their neighbours.

If you have made money your god then an abundance of it will make you happy and a lack of it will make you miserable. Do you think it is possible to reach a state of joy in your mind regardless of how much or how little money you have? So far, I have lived my life on a shoestring yet I know that I can live my truth and be financially independent. Money doesn't care who owns it or how it is acquired. Perhaps it is the lack of truth and focus upon survival that keeps one in lack…

I would like to now share with you a couple of experiences I've had. I realise this is going off track a bit but it's the only place I can fit them in!

Today is Thursday 2nd August 2001. On Monday of this week, I started a new job to add to my income as a manipulative therapist. The position was with a company called Sunshare Vacations, working as a travel sales consultant in one of their call centres. On the first day, my colleagues and I learned about the products the company sells and on the second day, we learned about their computer systems for doing bookings and managing incoming enquiries. On the third day, the training manager asked us if we had any problems thus far. Guess who said yes? One of the things the manager had taught us to do was to lie about seat availability when 'pitching' a customer on the phone. He said it was done to create a sense of urgency in the caller and it strongly encouraged them to book there and then. According to him, it was the company's practice and the only way they sold over the phone. I expressed my unwillingness to lie to their potential customers and he fired me on the spot! As I walked up the road from their offices, I realised I had acted impeccably and had got the wisdom from my 2-day travel sales career!

If you say you are truthful then you must eventually become it 100% of the time

The Blue Window

otherwise you are both a liar and a hypocrite. Most people are liars. Wisdom comes when the lies stop...

Later that day, I had a patient to see for manipulation of her neck. I had previously seen her on the Monday when I had successfully realigned her upper back but unfortunately her neck muscles were 'too tight' for manipulation of her vertebrae. This time, however, I was able to relax both her internal and external muscles and the necessary joint movement was done easily. She then mentioned, for the first time, that she was having pain in both her right wrist and right elbow. At the same time that I was treating her, we got into a deep conversation about her children seeing spirits in their home, which she and her husband didn't see. I was doing a general mobilisation technique on her wrist yet I was mainly focused on our conversation. Suddenly, the resistance that I could feel disappeared and then I moved to her elbow. I wasn't thinking about what I was doing; I was just doing it! We were both totally relaxed and engrossed in our conversation and we both felt the needed adjustment to her elbow.

Later in the evening, the lady called me to book her mother in for treatment. Then I had the most profound realisation. My spirit always knows exactly what to do and all I need to do is stop thinking about it and let the power within me do its work. It is a surrendering to and trusting in, the God within; and understanding that all healing comes from the God within. It is not me but I, the Father within me, that does the healing. When I allow my intellectual mind to interfere, then I actually hinder the healing process because truly my spirit knows it all. Providing my intent is righteous, then all I need do is become totally calm and the power of my spirit will reign. And the great spirit within me is the same great spirit that is within you.

The point of this chapter is this. If you don't go to the murk and mire of life, you're never going to know the higher orders of truth because this truth can only come from your own experiences. The world has many gurus with ulterior motives, hypocrites and philosophers who like the image of being enlightened but are they really enlightened? Or is their truth a limited one?

Please remember there is truth in everything. How much of life have you yet to experience? That is where your truth is. What you get to realise for yourself, whilst you're in flesh and blood, is the only thing you take with you in this life. In the afterlife, you can only ever go to where you know...

When Jesus died on the cross, it was symbolic. He was nailing that part of his personality, which comprised his altered-ego, to the cross. In other words, he was nailing all of his self-created, illusionary identities to the cross. His resurrection was his ascension. Time for another rethink?

The Blue Window

RESPONSIBILITY

The human 'condition' is a result of our inability to take responsibility for ourselves. Let us start by getting rid of a bit of confusion here. Most people think that being responsible is about being a good citizen, paying the bills on time and making sure their kids are fed, clothed and educated to do the same. Well, that's part of it but a very small part. There is a much greater responsibility; and that's the responsibility to yourself - to become a 'free thinker', to respect the free will of every individual and to live your truth.

At the moment in our society most of us are not free thinkers. Our minds have become the product and representation of mind control. For example, I asked a friend recently why she always had to watch Emmerdale Farm and she said, 'because it's always so 'real' life'. These programs do not depict real life; they help to create it! They are the cause; not the effect. Those who feast upon such a menu of low frequency 'social conscious' thoughts, will never be free thinkers.

Do we respect other people's free will? No! We murder them, we rape them, we beat them and we try to control and manipulate them. And our police do the same! I find it somewhat ironic that we don't take responsibility for ourselves yet we are always eager to take responsibility for everyone else's life! This is tyrannical behaviour and as subtle as it can be at times, we must start to see it as such.

We are truly only responsible for ourselves and our children, until they are of an age to say no and make their own decisions. Then we should readily let them go. However, because of our lack of wisdom, our mistaken sense of responsibility overspills into their lives. This is one of the many subtle forms of tyranny. And grandparents do the same thing; they are always eager to influence their grandchildren and try to impose their truth on them. When are we going to understand that this is a violation of the free will of another individual? We should never try to impose our truth on another for it is our truth based upon our experiences of life and not their truth.

Love is allowing others their truth and respecting their free will.

So why do we try to mould others to think like we do? Perhaps it's because we're not certain and resolute in our own truth? Ask yourself these questions. Are you entirely happy with yourself? Do you love yourself unconditionally? Do you live your truth or is your life just one big compromise? If your answer to any of these questions is no, then why would you want somebody else to think and be like you? Let them go and be free to live their own truth...

Now let's look at your responsibility to you. Your responsibility to you is to live

The Blue Window

your truth. That's it! But have you got a truth or have you lived somebody else's truth all of your life? You women are particularly good at this. I've lost count of the amount of women I've seen in my therapy practice that had thyroid problems because their lives were full of compromise, or they follow somebody else's truth, or they're just not hot enough to tell the truth. And they wonder why they're overweight, lack energy, have poor skin, circulation problems and get arthritis. I hope this is making sense to you. Men also have these problems, but it's normally because they're just outright liars or plain greedy. They like the image of giving but that's all it is.

The fifth seal in Ramtha's teachings is associated with living and speaking truth without duality. The thyroid gland is associated with the fifth seal. It will malfunction for one of three reasons (there are other reasons such as a dietary lack of iodine).

1 not living your truth
2 not telling the truth
3 not speaking your truth

Do you get sore throats or low neck pain? Contrary to your misconceived belief, your mind and your body are not separate. Now when I first say this to people they say they understand but they don't really. So let me say it again. Your mind and your body are sandwiched together and the jam in the sandwich is your emotional body. Did you get that? It is a scientific fact. Here's how it works again:

The conclusion of your thought processes, that which you often speak, is constantly being communicated to your body in two ways. Your brain communicates electrically via your central nervous system, messages to the cells of your body. Nerve impulses are electrical messengers that travel all the way down to your big toes via your sciatic nerves. Your brain also has a chemical factory called your endocrine system. This is a number of ductless glands that secrete chemicals, called neuro-peptides and hormones, across your brain and into your bloodstream. These are chemical messengers. They communicate information chemically to the organs and cells of your body and facilitate synaptic firing in your nerves.

Whether you believe it or not, your mind is the master and your body is its slave. Your body always conforms to your state of mind. It has no other choice! Therefore, the condition of your body will always reflect the condition of your mind. Go and look in the mirror. What is your body trying to tell you about the condition of your mind and the way you think?

If we only ever had loving thoughts then we would have perfect bodily health. Obviously, we all should be asking the question, what limiting attitudes am I

The Blue Window

allowing to run in my life? When we're busy being an emotional attitude then we're not being the observer of it, and thus we can't see it in us.

So what has this got to do with responsibility? Everything! Your every thought, whether you are conscious of it or not, is creating your reality and affecting the health of your body. Only you can take responsibility for your reality because you are the one creating it, whether you think you are or not. You are only the victim of external forces if you think you are and thus allow yourself to be.

Everything in your life is self-created.

Yet isn't it interesting how irresponsible we have become as a nation? We allow ourselves to be controlled and we abuse our bodies and then think it's somebody else's responsibility to fix the problems. What options has the poor doctor got? Drugs that at best alleviate the symptoms of our irresponsibility and make our recovery more comfortable. Bless them. If we don't start to change our attitudes then we're going to continue to play into the hands of the drug companies. Is it any wonder the drug companies are so rich and powerful?

When we start to take responsibility for ourselves, we learn how to care for our bodies by feeding our minds with purer and loftier thoughts. We change our lifestyle to reduce stress and we never compromise our health. Self-abuse is a lack of self-love. Doctors are redundant in a responsible society. In such a society we become our own physicians.

The poor state of a nations health is evidence of the degree of irresponsibility of its citizens.

When you don't speak your truth you affect the health of your body. What do you fear? The fear is affecting your body too! You can only hurt another's feelings if their feelings are there to be hurt, and their feelings are their responsibility not yours. So it is an issue for them, not you. Just speak your truth. If you are worried about the consequences as a result of speaking your truth, then why are you so insecure? What's the worst thing that can happen? Let it happen and you'll probably be pleasantly surprised at the outcome.

Are you living your truth? Do you rely on somebody else for your life? Will the other person die for you? Then why do you live for them? Believe it or not you have the free will to choose and you can always change your mind. It's your God given right. If you choose not to speak up for yourself then please don't talk behind another person's back or blame anyone else for your life, because it was always your option and your creation. Your reality will always reflect the decisions you make, including allowing others to make decisions for you.

The Blue Window

If you give your power away, if you give your free will away, and let somebody else make the decisions for you; then it was your choice to do that in the first place. Who are you living for? What about yourself? Can't find enough love for you? Now is a great time to start! Like the alcoholic, try taking one day at a time. How can I love myself just a little bit more today? That is the question to ask yourself everyday.

I also find it interesting how people lose themselves only to identify self in another. For instance, some parents shower their children with love and neglect themselves. What qualities do your children have that you perceive you don't have? To say that you love them and do not love yourself does not add up. You can only truly love another to the extent that you love yourself. Is it not the case that you're trying to live your life through them and for them? Such foolishness and evidence of your unbalanced state of mind. Wake up and realise that we're all the same, made of the same stuff and nobody is greater than anybody else; be they a child or an adult.

We were once as they are and the child is still within us, albeit under the surface of our conditioned responses. The child is still alive within all of us; we simply have to overcome the obstacles of our illusionary adult life and return to the child within. It's all just a state of mind.

The kingdom of Heaven is liken unto the little children – Jesus the Christ

There is a subtle balance. If you don't speak up for yourself and live your truth, you're always going to be a victim. And victims will always continue to be victimised. It's just the way it is. It's how the forces of energy work. When you think in polarities you attract to yourself the opposite of your polarity. The energy that you put out is always going to attract its opposite polarity, which in this case is tyranny. Victims attract tyrants and vice versa. On the other hand, if you are outspoken and try to impose your truth on others, then you are a tyrant. And you can only continue to play-out your little dramas (or big ones as the case may be) whilst you have a plentiful supply of victims or followers. Ironically, the tyrant will eventually experience the effects of their tyrannical behaviour.

So what is the answer to the above scenario? The answer is straight up the middle, where the pendulum sits still. It is not a compromised life; it is a greater truth.

The Blue Window

UNCONDITIONAL LOVE

There are distinctly two paths that we can take and live in our life. The first path is how we have been living our life to date. It is the path of our humanity and its unconscious emotional agreement with mind control. When Jesus the Christ created havoc in the marketplace, it was a deliberate demonstration to his disciples (enlightened rage). He said to them something like, 'when I act in this way I am being the Son of Man but when I perform miracles I am at once one with my Father in Heaven; I am the Son of God'. And his life demonstrated clearly the two different principles, obviously the former being the lower principle and the latter being the higher principle.

What determines which principle we enact in our life? It is simply the way we choose to think. If we allow our thoughts to be controlled then we're only ever going to know the lower principle - the Son and Daughter of Mankind. But if we change our minds and make a decision to be greater, then we can know the higher principle - the love of God. Making the decision to be greater is what starts the ball rolling...

The second path is actually our natural path, the conscious journey towards God. It is a journey into the hitherto unknown. It is making conscious that which is subconscious in us. It is letting go of every misconception we have ever known. It is growing up in consciousness, regardless of our age. It is learning to live our truth and becoming totally responsible. It is giving and giving and giving, without conditions. It is letting go of greed and self-interest. It is treating others as we would want them to treat us. It is letting go of our fears and becoming fearless. It is letting go of our illusions and the common diseases of the human mind, such as our attitudes of self-importance and our needs for acceptance and attention from others. It is reasserting our priorities in life and living for the acquisition of knowledge instead of our emotional addictions or how we look. It is being kind and generous without any ulterior motives. It is letting go of judgement and moving towards love. It is loving and respecting the free will of every individual and allowing them the freedom to express their truth. It is truly an uncompromised life. It is letting go completely. It is unconditional love. It is the love of a master.

Jesus the Christ never wanted to be idolised or worshipped. Through the example of his life he gave us the greatest gift of all, an *ideal* to live by. He said, 'follow me', he didn't say worship me! 'Make me your ideal' was his words and 'What I can do you can do greater'. This last quote was an evolutionary one. 'The father in me is the same father in you. I am the Son of God'. He never said I am the Son of God and you lot are all bastards of the universe! He recognised his own divinity and the equality of all of us. He sought to teach the ignorant mankind and to lift them to their higher principle. He failed miserably.

The Blue Window

GOD AND SCIENCE

I was provoked to write this chapter after watching a Channel 4 programme about testing God, scientifically.

To the dismay of you intellectuals, I am going to make this as simple as I can. There's no need to make God or science complicated when they really are very simple to understand.

Any scientist worth their salt will agree with the consensus of their profession, which states that 'everything in the universe is made of energy' and 'everything came from nothing in the first place'. Also, nothing that exists can be explained without including you and I in the equation because we are obviously a part of this universe, and how would we know that anything exists if we weren't observing it? We only *appear* to be separate from all things.

Let us take a closer look at the above statements. For everything to have come from nothing in the first place then obviously the nothing must have existed before everything! The nothingness must have at least contained the potentials for everything to be born from it. *Ramtha calls this one vast nothingness, the void, and he describes it as one vast nothing materially yet all things potentially.* The void cannot be quantified mathematically because what number could you give to an endless storehouse of unlimited potentials? Please give this some thought; your understanding of what is to follow will be enhanced if you can get your head inside the void, so to speak.

Unfortunately, we are programmed in our society to think that everything has a beginning and an end, but this is a very limiting way to think. Perhaps there never was a beginning and there is no end and the void always was, is and will be forever more. I hope this is making some sense to you.

Now, if everything in the universe is made of energy, then this energy can only have been born from the void and must have been contained within it; in whatever form. Indeed, it was and is, but the void has no form and its energy is asleep.

Before 'the beginning' then, there was the thought unawakened and the beginning was when it woke up. Through a process of contemplation, the void contemplated what it was and in doing so, inverted in upon itself and the child of the void was born. Thus *light was born from darkness*. Even the bible got that one correct! There is nothing evil about darkness; it just denotes 'not knowing' whereas light denotes 'knowing'. So, in essence, the grandparent of us all, woke up and started to create from itself...

The Blue Window

According to Ramtha, in our expansion from Point Zero, called the journey of involution, we created seven levels of reality. He uses the names of the bands of the electromagnetic spectrum to distinguish the different planes:

7 Infinite Unknown
6 Gamma Rays
5 X-Rays
4 Ultra Violet Rays
3 Visible Light
2 Infrared
1 Hertzian (mass)

All light, whether seen or unseen, can only exist in time because time is a creation in consciousness and light is energy. Consciousness and energy are the same thing. And everything, whether seen or unseen, is energy (confirmed by the scientists!). So the whole light spectrum comprises forms of energy and they exist in time and they were born from the darkness in the first place. Ramtha teaches that the big bang was not the beginning of creation but was the beginning of creation in the lower realms of time. The big bang was when the energy split into polarities and visible light was created in the journey of involution from the fourth down to the third level.

So does our earth also exist in the faster times of ultra violet light and x-rays? And how much life is in your microwave? Just because you don't see it doesn't mean it's not there! For example, Life in infrared is a billion times smaller than the life we normally see here. If we were all the size of Tom Thumb and everything else was scaled down relative to our new size, everything would still appear the same as it does now. The faster vibration we become the smaller and more powerful we are.

"Quantum Mechanics is the science of God. The discoveries to date make it just a branch of a much bigger tree" - Ramtha.

We cannot be separated from our environment because we are the ones observing it into being. Consciousness and energy is moulded by the mind of the observer ('Observer principle'). We are truly the moulders of the clay yet we still think we are the clay itself...

Our Scientists and Theologians seem to be worlds apart in their understanding of creation and evolution, but really they are closer than their own breath. The gulf is only there because they think of God as the 'Creator'. The result of such thinking is what we have got, believers and atheists. But when they understand that God is the creative source and we are the creating gods, then it will all start to make

The Blue Window

sense to them. And what holds all of creation together? Love. God is Love. It is the cosmic glue that loves everything into being and holds it all together.

God can only express unconditional love by allowing us to create whatever we want. If we are experiencing sorrow or suffering in our life then it is by our own hand and the result of our own lack of understanding. Everything is self-created. If you think it all just happened to you, then you are the one with a victim consciousness and you're going to attract more of the same!

The churches are full of victims and ignorant people. Fortunately, as consciousness is expanding, their numbers are falling. It's not that people no longer believe in God but rather they know that God is not what is portrayed by the various religions.

Ramtha teaches that the greatest church ever built is the human body because it houses a living god. Therein you will find your sanctuary with God. Bricks and mortar are manifestations of my lowest principle; my highest principle is in you.

In 1945, a Scroll was discovered at Nag Hamadi, which is described as 'The secret sayings of the living Jesus'. These are the hidden sayings that Jesus spoke.

"The Kingdom of God is inside you and all around you, not in buildings of wood and stone. Split a piece of wood and I am there. Whosoever discovers the meanings of these sayings will not taste death" - Jesus the Christ.

The Scroll, the Gospel of St. Thomas, has been claimed by scholars around the world to be the closest record we have of the actual words of Jesus. The Vatican refuses to recognise this Gospel and has described it as heresy.

If you want further information about this then may I suggest you start by taking a look at the film STIGMATA and then progress to the fabulous DVD's available from hamburgeruniverse.com

The Blue Window

BODY ENERGY CENTRES

The following is an excerpt taken, with permission, from the Ramtha book 'A Beginner's Guide to Creating Reality'. Its purpose is to clarify what Ramtha's truth is, in relation to the seven seals. If, throughout this book, I have diverted away from this core truth, then that is my understanding based upon my experiences and thus not necessarily Ramtha's truth.

"The seven seals in the human body are powerful energy centres that correspond to the seven planes of consciousness and energy. The bands are the way in which the physical body is held together according to these seals. In every human being there is energy spiralling out of the first three seals or centres. The energy pulsating out of these seals manifests itself as sexuality, pain or power. When the upper seals are unlocked, a higher level of awareness is activated.

The first three seals are the seals of sexuality, pain and suffering, and controlling power. These are the seals commonly at play in all of the complexities of the human drama.

The first seal is associated with the reproductive organs, sexuality and survival. It is related to the material or physical plane, which is the plane of the subconscious awareness and Hertzian frequency. It is the slowest and densest form of coagulated consciousness and energy.

The second seal is associated with the experience of pain and suffering and is located in the lower abdominal area. It is the plane of social consciousness and the infrared frequency band.

The third seal is associated with control, tyranny, victimization and power. It is located in the region of the solar plexus. The third plane is conscious awareness and the visible light frequency band. It is also known as the light plane and the mental plane. When the energy of the Blue Plane is lowered down to this frequency band, it splits into positive and negative polarity

The fourth seal is associated with unconditional love and the thymus gland. When this seal is activated, a hormone is released that maintains the body in perfect health and stops the aging process. The fourth plane of existence is the realm of bridge consciousness and ultraviolet frequency. This plane is also called the Blue Plane or the plane of Shiva (Shiva being the destroyer of the old and creator of the new). In this plane, energy is not yet split into positive and negative. Any lasting changes or healing of the physical body must be changed first at the level of the fourth plane and the Blue Body.

The Blue Window

The fifth seal is associated with the thyroid gland and with speaking and living the truth without duality. The fifth plane of existence is the plane of super-consciousness and x-ray frequency. It is known as the Golden Plane or Paradise.

The sixth seal is associated with the pineal gland. The reticular formation that filters and veils the knowingness of the subconscious mind is opened when this seal is activated. The sixth plane is the realm of hyperconsciousness and the gamma ray frequency band. In this plane the awareness of being one with the whole of life is experienced.

The seventh seal is associated with the crown of the head and the pituitary gland. It represents the attainment of enlightenment. The seventh plane is the plane of ultra-consciousness and the Infinite Unknown frequency band. This plane is where the journey of involution began. It was created by Point Zero when it imitated the act of contemplation of the Void and the mirror or secondary consciousness was created. A plane of existence or dimension of space and time exists between two or more points of consciousness. All the other planes were created by slowing down the time and frequency band of the seventh plane.

Point Zero refers to the original point of awareness created by the Void through its act of contemplating itself. Point Zero is the original child of the Void, the birth of consciousness. The Void is defined as one vast nothing materially, yet all things potentially. Ramtha also calls it the Mother/Father Principle. In Ramtha's teachings, the Source and God the creator are not the same. God the creator is seen as Point Zero and primary consciousness but not as the Source, or the Void, itself".

End of excerpt.

Also, in the same book, Ramtha describes how the seven energy centres are linked to bands of light that some people call an aura. The physical body itself is a frequency of light that is so slow that it appears solid. It is the Hertzian frequency of light. The bands of light surround the physical body and kind of sit upon one another. Each band of light interacts with the physical body carrying with it thoughts that are consistent with its frequency. For example, the infrared frequency band carries different kinds of thoughts to that of ultraviolet light.

I am now going to give some examples, from my own life, of the kind of thoughts each energy centre receives, from consciousness, for onward transmission to the brain, for computation and comparison with one's memory. Some people call these energy centres chakras but I will refer to Ramtha's description – seals.

The Blue Window

The First Seal

This relates to the physical body itself and indeed everything that appears physical. This energy centre sits at the base of the spine and is linked to the sexual organs. The consciousness that it carries is dominated by thoughts of sex, survival, procreation and physical appearance. So when our thoughts are dominated by how we look, sexual desires, issues of survival, we are said to be body-conscious.

Your reality will always reflect your most dominant thoughts. Are you a body-conscious entity? Are you therefore really no greater than the animal kingdom?

The Second Seal

The consciousness that is carried to the brain through this centre is fearful thoughts associated with pain and suffering. It is representative of the human emotional condition. All emotional reactions are fear based i.e. there is a lack of knowledge. When you are reacting emotionally, you are experiencing thoughts that have come through this energy centre and of course those that you have associated with in your past - your memories.

Memories are like shadows that flicker upon a great fire. You are the great fire that created the shadows! Is your energy held in the second seal? Are you no more than an emotional bag of chemicals? That's all an emotion is - a chemical reaction in your body precipitated by the way you choose to think.

Any emotional reaction, no matter what it is, is evidence of your own lack of understanding. It is only knowledge that dissipates the fear. If your life is full of pain, suffering or fear, it is because it serves you to be that way. Maybe it's the only way you can get attention, affection and your emotional needs met?

The Third Seal

This is the centre of *raw* power and is linked with the adrenal glands at the Solar Plexus area of the body. Notice I said raw power and not real power. This is the consciousness of tyranny and victimisation.

Tyranny has many faces and its subtleties will always amaze you. When you assume responsibility for others (with the exception of your own small children), you are experiencing a subtle form of tyranny. When you are giving compassion to another person, you are experiencing a subtle form of tyranny. The compassion is what the victim needs for attention. On the other hand, is the one who gives the responsibility of their life away to other people. They can then blame other people when undesirable things happen to them.

The Blue Window

The irony of the third seal is all tyrants eventually become victims and vice versa. This applies to individuals and any collective consciousness. For example, America has become the victim of its own tyrannical consciousness. They are always poking their noses into 'other peoples' business under the guise of peace, but with the ulterior motive being control. If you try to impose your will on others you will eventually be victimised. That's just the way energy works on this level. The consciousness is polarised, it always moves towards balance. That's why the fighting continues around the world. One act that is not motivated by love will always be balanced by an opposing act that is not motivated by love. So what is the answer? It is obviously to love one another.

When we meet violence with violence we will always fuel more violence. If total domination ever occurs, which is what the controlling elite want, then we will never know true freedom on this planet. It is only with unconditional love that we can heal the wounds of the past. Not everybody wants to see women treated worse than dogs in the street and see such a flagrant abuse of basic human rights. And not everybody wants a materialistic world that prefers fashion to God and prefers to pollute the environment rather than take reduced profits or even losses...get my drift?

I want to make my position clear here. I am not for or against America or their people. I am not for or against any country. If one country can develop a nuclear arsenal of weapons to protect its borders, its beliefs, its way of life and its religious, political and economic systems: then is it not reasonable that all countries should have the same right? We either live with a nuclear threat or we ban these weapons universally. I obviously would prefer the latter option. The same yardstick should apply to all disarming. It's no good just asking the Republicans in Ireland to disarm in the name of peace without asking the Loyalists and even the British forces for that matter!

A few years ago the ex Prime Minister of New Zealand, Mr David Lange, came to London and successfully argued for the banning of nuclear weapons, based upon their immorality. New Zealand subsequently became a nuclear free zone and a neutral country. If we all had the same attitude, it would be a huge step in the right direction for global peace. It is not acceptable for America to argue for such weapons to exist on the basis that other countries might use them against America, when we know that America is a country that has used them offensively. Tend your own backyard first lest you have dualistic standards and hypocrisy.

Terrorism is not the cause of the problems we are currently experiencing but is the effect of a tyrannical consciousness that is trying to control the planet. The real tyrants are not those that are shoved in our faces by our media, but are the elitist families of mainly bankers who go about their business away from public

The Blue Window

scrutiny. We are both the victims of terrorism and the prime cause of it, because we are not bringing the real tyrants into public view and accountability. The global situation is only going to change when we all start to change our attitudes...

The Fourth Seal

This energy seal is the consciousness of unconditional love. It is linked to the thymus gland that sits next to the heart. No surprise is it really? This is an energy that is not polarised; it is wholesome. Therefore, when we give love unconditionally that's what we attract. Unfortunately, most people haven't opened up this energy centre because they haven't taken the time to contemplate what it would be like to love unconditionally. They are too addicted to their emotional dramas and thus there is no room for the greater light of love to exist around them.

Using Ramtha's definitions of the seals, we can see that the human condition is currently held in the first three seals. We are always playing-out some kind of emotional drama. If we're not being tyrannical we're playing victim or being an emotional wimp. Then there are those of us whose consciousness is still stuck in between our legs! Bodily gratification, what we look like, what we're eating and who we're sleeping with; dominate our thoughts. There's nothing wrong with this; we just should know where we're at on a scale of one to seven - one!

Take a good look at our society. We are all victims because we are dependent on the government, the local authorities, the supermarkets, the oil companies, the pharmaceutical companies and other multi-national companies. Most people are totally dependent. This may give you a feeling of freedom but it's not true freedom. What would you eat if there was no food in your supermarkets? How would you get to work without a supply of fuel? What are you going to drink if main water supplies become polluted? How are you going to heat your home if there is no mains gas or electricity? How are you going to cope without your weekly fix off the doctor? How are you going to make ends meet without the government handouts?

We have all allowed ourselves to become dependent and thus vulnerable.

We have given the responsibility for our lives away to a government to look after us. And we vote for the party that we think is going to look after us the best! Take the farmers and the BSE crisis as an example. They blamed the government because they wanted the 'clean up' and compensation handouts. I don't see that the BSE epidemic was the government's fault! As a nation we have completely given our power away. When we are not being cared for adequately, we blame those who we have given our power away to, and this makes us victims. We are not the sovereign, powerful, responsible beings that we could be.

The Blue Window

The 'powers that be' are happy to assume responsibility for us because they revel in the illusionary power that control brings; and of course the benefits of having a captive market - the obscene wealth that capitalism brings to the few that are material successes.

It is our victim attitudes and our emotional dependency that has created the materialistic system in the West. Capitalism caters for our creature comforts and serves the majority of consumers but at what cost? The by-products of our consumer-driven society are killing our planet!

We have become nothing more than image-conscious consumers. Of course the governments want full employment! It keeps our focus to where they want it - consuming more goods and services, making more profit for the banks and multi-national companies.

Because of our own greed and dependence, we have helped to construct a monster of a society that is killing the very platform upon which we live. If we continue in this vein our future is clear; we will not have a healthy environment in which to play-out our emotional experiences. It is up to each and every one of us to change our attitudes. We must become more responsible for ourselves and less dependent on our society for what we think we need. Becoming more sovereign is the way forward...

If we do not change our behaviour we will face a colossal natural disaster.

If there is ever a huge natural disaster, you won't be able to look to the government for a handout. They probably won't exist on the surface anymore! If you don't make provisions for yourself and this occurs, then only you can take responsibility for your lack of action. You can no longer hide behind your own ignorance now that you have the knowledge.

You may say, 'what has all this got to do with the fourth seal of unconditional love?' Becoming sovereign in your attitude and providing for yourself is not a survivalist attitude but rather it is an act of self-love, the greatest love there is. People are generally preserved by nature if they have taken action to preserve themselves.

So what is unconditional love? It is a giving without any conditions whatsoever. There must not be any ulterior motives. A good example would be anonymous giving. The giving of knowledge that can help the soul of another person is another good example. This book is an act of love because it gives to you knowledge without any conditions whatsoever. And you loved yourself enough to buy it!

The Blue Window

Love often works in mysterious ways; it is not always obvious. For instance, deliberately severing a tie with another can be an act of love towards them, as well as self-love, although they probably won't see it that way. True love is not emotional string pulling, enslavement or image-conscious ideals that we lay upon each other. It is not the conditional love that we experience as human love.

If your partner suddenly changed and became antagonistic towards you, and behaved in a manner that you considered to be socially unacceptable, would your love for them be dented or would it be constant? True love is constant and all allowing. No matter how we choose to behave, God still loves us all. That is unconditional love. It is the love that allows us to continue to exist, no matter how degraded our behaviour has been.

It is the destiny of humanity to live as super-conscious, loving beings. It is the only way we can ever achieve true freedom and peace on earth. I am hoping this book will help inspire people to start the process of personal transformation. It is an alchemical process that transmutes the lead of human frailty into the gold of spiritual truth. Eventually, I hope we can all become super-conscious beings.

The introduction of ID cards is evidence that we are all physically different. Our eyes and fingerprints are all different. Did you know that no two people have exactly the same genetic code? Every one of us is special. So why is it most of us pass this world without leaving any evidence of being here apart from a gravestone? Most people are forgotten very quickly. You're not going to go down in herstory for being a mother unless you were mother Theresa! And do you think history is going to remember you for your DIY skills? What legacy do you want to leave? It's never too late to make a difference...

We live in a world to where we act in a similar way to others, so that we are acceptable to them and society in general. We look for acceptance and approval from outside of ourselves. Our mental conditioning has developed us into being no more that social creatures. We find common ground with other people so as to be 'cool', instead of pursuing the uncommon in us, which will make us great. We agree and conform like the herd mentality of a sheep; not even aware that the eagles watch us from above.

When we become an individual we no longer look outside of ourselves for acceptance, for love, approval, feeling special, self-importance, attention, compassion, motivation, permission, authority or God. We eventually learn that it is all within us and it has always been that way. It takes a brave person to separate themselves from the herd mentality.

The Blue Window

The Fifth Seal

This energy centre is linked to the thyroid gland. It is the great truth gland. I have already spoken about truth so I'll only do a quick recap. Truth is an absolute consciousness, meaning that you can't cheat it because it will always catch you out. In other words, you can't play games with it and you can't bend it without it being thrown back in your face! You either are it or you're not; it's as simple as that. Mastery of this level of consciousness means being truthful 100% of the time. A momentary lapse is a fracturing of your energy. Here are some of the reasons why you are not a truthful being:

You are a liar (the white ones count too).
You compromise your life for other people.
You portray one motive but live another.
You never really know the person you are living with because they are just feeding your emotional needs and you are feeding theirs. The basis of the relationship is an unconscious agreement to feed each other's emotions.
You commit adultery, if not physically then in your mind.
You act contrary to what you know your truth is.
You live your truth through the eyes of another thus you are living their truth.
You say one thing yet you do another.
You are a hypocrite.
You fantasise about other people instead of living your fantasies.
You follow your emotions instead of your intuition.
You do not act when you know you should.
You allow your fear to hold you back.
You make excuses. They are all the same.
You tell people what you think they want to hear instead of the truth.
You live for the acceptance, approval and recognition of others.

You do not become a truthful being overnight. It takes a long time to fully develop your golden body. A person who has mastered truth is said to be a super-conscious being. Mastery of this level puts you on the road to greatness. It is your personal truth that sets you free. Can you imagine living in a society of loving, truthful beings? Do you share my vision?

The Sixth Seal

This is linked to the Pineal gland. What follows is only partly my truth because I have yet to experience all of it. The sixth seal is the home of the Shaman, the Seer, the Witchdoctor, the Wizard, the Genius, the Healer and the Magician. Phenomenon experienced include out-of-body travel, being in two places at one time, remote viewing, miraculous healing, instant manifestation, levitation,

The Blue Window

innovative invention, time-travel, bio-relocation, changing embodiment at will, seeing around corners, dimensional hearing, prophetic vision, telepathy, magical flight, the ability to grow wings etc....

The following is what I have realised to date, that we must develop if we don't already posses:

An indomitable will.
A relentless determination to continue to go forward.
A desire that is greater than all of your emotional addictions.
A willingness to leave the past behind forever, without longing or regret.
Discipline, Patience and being Calm at all times.
Outstanding focus upon dreaming new thoughts into being.
A relaxed, concentration of focus upon your dreams
An active not passive attitude. No action equates no movement of energy.
The love of self.
The state of being absolutely truthful at all times.
An unquenchable thirst for new knowledge.
An open mind and the acceptance of your own unlimited potentials.
The willingness to face and overcome your fears.
The courage to face adversity and to cease repetitive known experiences.
A thorough knowledge of Quantum Mechanics.
A mind that is dominated by your loftiest goals.
The realisation that there is nowhere to hide and nowhere to go, except within.
The courage to betray yourself and expose the lies.
The ability to hold your focus on your desires. An untrained mind will always wander.
The knowingness to surrender to the God within you, the source of all creation.

The Seventh Seal

The Pituitary is the master gland and the seventh seal is the crowning centre of Christ consciousness. The energy at this level is so fast that it is known as Infinite Unknown. Only one who experiences it can describe the consciousness and even then any words used would carve away at its glory. Please think for a moment. All that we know about God and the enigma known as Christ is a religious teaching. What if the religions have lied to us? Here is what I know about the qualities of a Christ. We can all attain this level of understanding and experience the loftiest realities here on earth. This is creating Heaven on Earth:

I am God; my Father and I are one mind.
I am non-judgemental.
I am pure, unconditional love.

The Blue Window

I am without ulterior motive.
I am uncompromised in my life.
I am unlimited mind.
I am a multidimensional being
I am the master of all time.
I am accountable to none other than my mother/father in Heaven.
I am liken unto the little children.
I love the God in me with all of my heart, with all of my soul and with all of my mind.
I love myself as I love my God and I love my neighbour as I love myself.
I am loving and truthful always.

Finally, here is a quote from my other book entitled 'Christ Consciousness 101 reasons Why':

"We are intelligent energy surrounding intelligent energy, with limited personal expression due to our own attitudes, which are both in-bred and the result of mind accumulation that keeps getting environmentally triggered. Said another way, we are spirit & soul surrounding body & personality; the latter being dominant and the outward expression of our attitudes and our habitual behaviour.

Originally, our body & personality grew out of our spirit & soul (for a divine purpose); but we got confused by identifying ourselves with the former instead of the latter - a mistaken identity and the reason we are known by enlightened beings as the forgotten gods.

The body and its emotionally-based personality are closely related. At best, a health-conscious personality can add a few years of life to its vehicle, but ultimately they cannot save each other. Ironically, it is this personality that final brings down the body.

So what is Christ consciousness? Well work it out for yourself! If a Christ is a being who has the mind to be able to make the body immortal then obviously he/she has to destroy that which destroys the body! Christ consciousness is the complete removal of the personality's emotional-hooks into the body. It is effectively the death of the lower personality; it is the death of body-emotional-mind consciousness.

What comprises the nature of this personality? It is all the unloving aspects that arise from the illusion of separation. Christ consciousness, on the other hand, is the full personal realisation of the higher truth and the simultaneous resurrection of the true self-identity."

The Blue Window

EVOLUTION

We obviously have a problem with reincarnation because (according to Ramtha) we have been reincarnating here for 10.5 million years and our consciousness is still stuck in the first three seals! That means we have been repeating the same kind of consciousness for 10.5 million years! Is that not emotional addiction?

A responsible parent is one who has acquired a certain level of knowledge, which allows them to interact with the soul of their child. When they reach a certain level of understanding, they can help to free their child from his or her genetic impediments, and without subjecting the child to further limiting thoughts.

So how many times have we been married? How many lovers and mistresses have we had? How many children have we given birth to through our many lives? How many times have we had sex? How many times have we come through the birth canal? How many times have we died? And why do we fear death when it is an experience we have every lifetime? It's all just a lack of knowledge...

Here we are again, stuck on this backward planet, the same souls sporting different bodies with different faces. The same old drama with new scenery. The environment is constantly changing but the drama stays essentially the same. We, as human thinkers, have stagnated. We just 'tread water' and 'suck air' until we die, and then we come back for another dose of recycled ignorance! And the best about it is - we think we're so great!!

Ramtha explains in his wonderful teachings on the 'Planes of Bliss': In the light you undergo a review of your life and you get to see the folly of your existence here. You see the opportunities for change that you missed and you see your self-abuse and the less than impeccable way you have behaved and treated others. It's not that you have ever done anything wrong but that you don't learn from your mistakes and change your behaviour accordingly. Whenever you change your mind and thus your behaviour, you have owned that aspect of your life and it no longer forms part of your 'unfinished business' here. This becomes obvious to you in your 'Light Review'.

Our unfinished business is what causes us to return here, time and time again. How many more lives are we going to spend stuck on this confused world? We keep going to the light and coming back, going to the light and coming back...

"There is a nebula called the City of Light – it is an actual place – and the most valuable beings in all of the cosmos come from the City of Light. In other words, there is no night time in this place. It is all bathed in a golden light. It is spectacular! What are the animals and plants like? Those who depend upon being

The Blue Window

bathed in a golden light. And what about the beings that are there? Beings that live with a golden light and are made of it. This is a nebula way out there – way, way from the earth. It was often confused that that was where Yeshua Ben Joseph went, but he did go there and he resides there. All masters go there." - Ramtha

Each environment offers the incoming soul different opportunities. What we get to experience in the future depends upon what we know now and in the future.

According to Ramtha, souls who are on the planes of bliss, who plan to return to the earth, get to wait in long queues for conception of a baby's body to occur. There is apparently a shortage of new babies to accommodate the vast number of incoming souls waiting to come back here. Some souls come back to the same family because the family perpetuates a mindset and thus the genetic pool continues to be suitable for the incoming soul.

In the case of my children, they were conceived shortly after each of my grandparents died, so both my grandparents had a new body available to come back quickly. Knowing them as my grandparents and as my children, has given me a wonderful insight into what their genetic encumbrances are. Through careful thought I am helping them to unchain their minds, thus paving the way for the return of my own parents, if they can overcome some of their genetic impediments. This is responsible evolution.

In other civilisations, such as the races of the Pleiades, they apparently live for hundreds of years and when it is time to make the transition, they lay down the body and consciously move to a child's body from their offspring. Schooling and education are ongoing parts of their community. They understand that their children will get to know more than they know and they will make the transition to be taught by their children. This is beautiful evolution.

The Pleiadians will only visit us when they are convinced we have moved to a higher, more loving consciousness. At the moment they see us as nothing more than primitive people. And they are correct in their observation. Just take a look at what's happening in our world at any given moment. Although the majority of us are basically good people with good intentions, there is obviously a minority who are unquestionably insane!

I started writing this chapter earlier this morning (28/09/01) and I've just taken a break to pop down to my local bank. Whilst paying in my partner's daily receipts, I was chatting to the female bank teller. I forget now what I said to her but she responded with the classic, 'I'm only human you know'. I said, 'I beg to differ with you on that point' and I said, 'with the way we are behaving in the world at the moment, I would be proud if somebody was to call me an alien!'

The Blue Window

It's fitting that I've mentioned the blue-body races because their consciousness is obviously 'beyond the light'. We should never want to go back to the light just to return to a crippled consciousness, when we know we can go beyond it and live in peace and true freedom. When we become responsible for our own evolution, we realise that every thought we allow to manifest in our life, counts in the light of all eternity. We are eternal beings and this is how we should think of ourselves.

Leonardo de Vinci once said, "Consider the end first". It doesn't matter how you've lived your life to date. Dream about how you would like to live it from now on and the exquisite being you would like to become. If you hold onto your dreams, you will eventually experience them. Your dominant thoughts will continue to be your future reality. They may not manifest in this lifetime but that doesn't matter. Please remember you are an eternal being and only you can carve up your dreams with the sword of doubt.

As for me, my dream is firmly placed on my timeline. There is no doubt in my mind that I will achieve it. It may not occur in this lifetime but if I keep walking forward, as I am doing, then there's no reason why it won't happen.

What are your dreams? Become like the little child again and create those pictures in your mind. They are more real than the reality you are currently looking at. Your dreams are your future days; please design them beautifully.

I find that people struggle to understand the nature of reality and to understand this world as a grand illusion. They think that it is very real and fixed and nothing exists beyond it. But this reality is only what you perceive it to be through the senses of your body. So whilst you're in the physical body, everything that you see, smell, touch, feel and hear is real to you. But when you 'fall off your perch' and are caught up in a new embodiment, in a faster time; then you are unable to perceive this world. As frustrating as this may be to you, this world will no longer be real to you. What is real is your own experience. Every level of creation is real whilst you're experiencing it, but it's also a grand illusion, created for the purpose of emotionally experiencing it. There is only really one true reality and that is the love that holds it all together - God.

When you realise the above it's quite a shock to your system because it pulls the plug on your altered-ego and starts to break down all of those illusionary identities you've held about yourself. It's time to grow up and realise that you're not a body but you are the intelligence that subconsciously controls your body. You have the free will to think what you want but if your conscious thoughts are not in alignment with the upper four seals, as described earlier, then your body will atrophy and eventually die. Your immortality is in your own hands. It has always been that way.

The Blue Window

I have realised I am creating my own reality by the way I choose to think here and now. However I choose to live is up to me. As long as I take responsibility for my thoughts and actions I will never again be a victim. I take full responsibility for what I have written in this book. It was my choice to write it.

Why did I choose to write this book? It was because I wanted to make a difference and I wanted to give people the opportunity to know what I know. I have come to this planet to learn the Great Work and what I am learning is that I am the Son of God and you are the same as I am. It has taken me many years of pain and pleasure to reach this juncture in my life. I share with you in one book what has been a huge investment in learning on my part. It really is my pleasure to know that you are reading my words. It is for you they are written. There is something for every person in this book and I hope you will join with me to spread the word.

The other reason for my writing to you is that I can no longer stand back and watch silly little boys play with their big toys. They are so pathetic. The day they realise that love is the answer is the day they will grow up. If we are going to continue to have lethal weapons then every one of us has the God-given right to carry such weapons for self-protection. Whilst we've got lethal weapons then there is always going to be some idiot that will use them. For some to carry weapons and others not to have them just enforces control and that is not love. If we want to live in a loving, free environment then all lethal weapons should be banned universally. And there should be no need for law enforcement agencies either. It is the third seal consciousness that is currently creating conditions here.

To pull ourselves out of the nosedive and to maintain a cruising altitude we have got to up the level of consciousness that prevails here.

The Blue Window

SEX AND RELATIONSHIPS

I thought I'd best write this chapter because we seem to be so preoccupied with sex and relationships. If you're not broadminded or you're a bit of a prude then you best skip this chapter because I'm going to tell it how I really see it.

If this is the first chapter you've come to then it just goes to show you where your consciousness is held! May I suggest you at least read the previous chapter 'Body Energy Centres' before you continue with this one. I'm going to try and relate the body energy centres with the sexual experience in a light-hearted way.

The First Seal

Picture this. You're a teenager again and you're taking your last holiday with your parents. You've grown up to be a fine young specimen of your gender and you're aptly displaying your vital statistics down on the beach. It's a beautiful day and there are plenty of other fine young specimens around. Your adult faculty has recently been revealed to you but you haven't really done much about it, other than those solitary moments of indiscretion.

You take a fancy to another body and you unknowingly make it obvious. Coincidentally, or so you think, their badminton shuttlecock lands in your lap! Your eyes meet and that's it - love at first sight (lust at first sight!). When your mum's not looking you're off, out of sight, down the other end of the beach with body perfect.

You're holding hands walking towards the sand dunes. Are you being led or are you doing the leading? Who cares! Are they thinking the same as you? They must be, you hope. You're nervous but willing to experience. You both go deep into the sand dunes. Are you going to get caught? You secretly hope so but not before your first moment in the sun!

Sorry but I'm going to have to stop there. I'll leave the rest to your own fantasy or memory as the case may be. I'm not going to allow you to 'get off' on my words! I'm sure you won't have a problem completing the rest of the scene...

Every experience we have should be like a virgin experience. Christ is born of a virgin. However, we become emotionally entangled through repetition of the same experiences and by our automatic mind-association with them.

The first seal sexual experience is not without emotion. Evidence of this is that all memories are stored in the body emotionally. Every physical experience is therefore an emotional hit on the body. The first two seals are only distinguishable

The Blue Window

by the fact that we find it difficult and undesirable to have sex when we are in pain or are suffering.

A lustful person who is nothing more than a sexual predator is said to be a first seal entity. Most young men are no greater than the first seal experience. They've just got to have it and it doesn't particularly matter who with! The fire in their loins is so great that it's convenient if you come along at the right time otherwise the nearest loo will do. That's about as good as it gets at this level. Don't kid yourself that you mean anything to them. They don't care. To them, you're just a willing body that's going to satisfy them.

I know of some women like this too. They have lowered themselves to the level of us men. They have no love for themselves and obviously no respect for their bodies. Fortunately, most women are more than their animal counterparts.

The Second Seal

This seal represents pain and suffering, so what could represent a painful sexual experience? Well, some people voluntarily have sex even though it causes them pain. I can't imagine why, other than they have given their power away completely to their partner. Then of course we have rape and sadomasochistic perversions. Then we have those who take advantage of another's suffering. In their astounding wisdom they think that a partner who's being emotional just needs a good seeing to. They prey upon the obvious weakness of another, not realising that they, themselves, are their weakest in the same moment. Maybe the partner's show of emotion is the subtle power of one who knows just how to keep you where they want you - grounded in your first seal.

The Third Seal

Women are nearer to God because, in evolutionary terms, most of them start from this higher 3rd rung of the 7-step evolutionary ladder. I have departed from Ramtha's teachings here, as you will see at the end of this chapter by reading the contribution made by Mike Wright of Ramtha's School of Enlightenment.

As you should now know, the third seal is the place of *raw* power. And women are experts at wielding power over men. They are clever, they are cunning and they are seductresses. They know just how to 'pull um'. It's a shame that it's the only power most of them seem to have. A powerful woman can easily control a weak man. It's the fanny trap. A weak man is easily beguiled by the temptations of the seductress. When the man falls into the trap he becomes the victim of the tyrant. He is then at his weakest moment. Few men are strong enough to resist such a woman.

The Blue Window

The powerful woman struggles with the most basic man because he just doesn't care - he'll shag anything! She also struggles with the powerful man because such a man can subvert her at times. She wants good-looking victims to achieve her life of compromise. The powerful man, on the other hand, is not really a sexual man. Sexual activity to him is normally just an extension of his business life - another conquest. Only the most powerful woman can stand up to him and then we have fireworks. It's a battle for control and both are swinging back and forth between tyranny and victimisation. And the games they play beggar belief. Two tyrants become fixated on trying to teach each other a lesson or trying to get 'one over' the other. What a waste of valuable energy.

A quick recap before we move on up. Where sex and relationships are concerned, most men are caught in the first seal experience. Their passion in life is definitely for sex. On the other hand, a truly spiritual man will not be found in the first seal but in the fourth and upwards. And most women, in evolutionary terms, are closer to God. Their passion is generally not for sex; they are powerful beings who compromise their truth for survival. They are conditioned to think that their survival involves having a man in their life and they're 'lost' without one. They have a head start in evolutionary terms, yet instead of moving on and up the evolutionary ladder, they anchor down for survival and meet the man in the first seal experience.

I have had married women say to me about their relationships with their husbands, 'where the sex is concerned I can take it or leave it'. One therefore has to ask the question, 'if that is the case then why do you continue to take it?' Rare is the woman who lives her truth, because most women compromise to perpetuate an illusionary lifestyle. And if they are not careful the only difference between them and a prostitute is the prostitute is being truthful!

If you are struggling in a sexual relationship then you need to take a look at your own attitudes. And what does your partner mirror to you that you don't currently own in yourself? Find out the real reasons for the relationship; then you will have your truth and you will know where to go from there.

The Fourth Seal

True love doesn't exist in the first three energy centres. What we know as human love is a conditional love. It is 'I love you providing you continue to meet my ideal for you but don't bank on it if you change and break the mould I have caste you in. When I say I love you I really mean I need you. You are to fit in with my image and its needs otherwise I'm going to get emotional and pull you into line'.

Contrary to the above, when we love unconditionally; we love everyone the same.

The Blue Window

We can no longer differentiate between one person and another where love is concerned. This can be very disconcerting, especially where sex is concerned, because it is easy to confuse sexual interest with true love and affection towards another. Love and sex are not the same thing, but they can easily be confused when one is treading new ground and evolving. The old attitudes and emotions of the past will bite at your heels for a while until you fully understand the difference and accept your new view as the way forward. Only then will the demons of your past finally leave you. Indeed, it is your focus upon them that keeps them alive in you.

So can lovemaking play a part in a relationship where two people love each other unconditionally? I sense that any copulation becomes an extension of the expression of love that two highly evolved people share. Sex is not the reason for the relationship nor is any form of emotional or financial dependency. There is also an absence of fighting for control or competitiveness. There is just an unconditional acceptance, giving, allowing and encouragement for one another to change and grow beyond previous boundaries.

This new kind of relationship is first and foremost a meeting of two evolving minds and is viewed as such. The meeting of body parts is no longer important, although lovemaking can be a natural occurrence for two spiritually-minded people. Acts of lovemaking therefore become acts of mutual giving that extend the love two people share and freely express. Fourth seal lovemaking bears little resemblance to lustful sex, emotional dependency and the control dramas found in the first three seals.

The Fifth Seal

This is the energy centre that represents living your truth without duality or compromise. In developing the great golden body of truth, you can have as many relationships as you want, as long as you always tell the truth! In saying this, I must emphasise that a person living from this seal would find that most relationships compromise their truth, and thus they are unlikely to be in one. If they have a partner it will certainly be a monogamous situation...

There is nothing immoral about having many different partners as long as you are truthful with all of them. Immorality stems from being untruthful. Being truthful is the great regulator; it automatically engenders a state of morality. The sexual predator exists in a state of untruthfulness because a truthful predator is socially unacceptable and would therefore not attract their prey. I remember once having several girlfriends on the go at the same time. Had I told them the truth I would have blown them all out of the water. Such an existence coexists with lies. It is not the kind of behaviour tolerated by a truthful person.

The Blue Window

It is obviously far less stressful and potentially healthier to have one partner at a time. Being essentially single and changing partners every now and then is far less compromising, and allows one to be truthful with all of them. There is nothing wrong with having many partners - it is, in fact, you looking for your perfect reflection. You are looking for love (God) unknowingly.

The pursuit of getting love from other people is often confused with sex and all that is found is a mirroring of one's own lack. If you live your life in such a fashion then it may indeed be your truth but please don't carry your old relationships around with you because your future lovers are not going to want to hear about your past ones. It often takes a long time for people to realise they can only find true love within themselves.

Now to the couples, heterosexual, homosexual, lesbians, confused, married or otherwise. If you are truthful to your partner and you never fantasise about other people; then you are one of a splendid few. However, most people have fantasies, which if they don't live-out, they become the basis of their next life. Please remember that all thoughts are real and if not experienced, remain on your time-line, until you have got the wisdom from such experiences. If you are living with a partner but fantasising about other people; then sooner or later you had better decide whether your truth is in your relationship or with your demons. Once you have decided what your truth is, then it is simply a matter of being true to it.

If you're in a relationship and you think you've got the best of both worlds by staying and having affairs with other people, instead of doing the decent thing and leaving; then you should think again: you're affairs may represent your truth and your relationship is probably a lie. Either way around, you are compromised and a liar.

To be a truthful person, your actions must marry your spoken word; otherwise you are a house divided against itself. This not only applies to your sexual relationships, but to all areas of your life. In truth, there is no room for any porky pies whatsoever. You are either a truthful person or you're not. It is impossible to cheat consciousness at this level.

Your mastery of the fifth seal will take you a long time because your deep-seated attitudes are the core of your untruthfulness. It will take you a long time to unseat them and it is always with a degree of suffering. But if you change and keep polishing your act, eventually you will shine like the diamond you are. So be it!

The Sixth Seal

Can sex be enjoyed at this level? I am hypothesising now but to think it couldn't would be a limitation in one's mind. As I understand this level of consciousness, it is almost unlimited in its point of view. Probably the best way of answering the question is with another question. Did Einstein think about sex all day long or virtually not at all? You see, it's all about where your focus is. Your reality will always reflect where your focus is.

A masterful being can lower their energy for the purpose of lovemaking at any time, but why would they want to do that when they are in the rapture and ecstasy of creating genius in the moment? The sixth seal is the realm of the supernatural and paranormal experiences that can only be achieved through dedication and a one-pointed, concentrated focus upon one's goals. Apparently there is an ecstasy that exists in the mind that is far greater than the physical orgasm...

To seat our energy in the sixth seal therefore requires a stance against the lower energy centres and that obviously confirms there is a price to pay for greatness. We will never find greatness in the humdrum mediocrity of the human condition.

To aspire to the upper echelons of consciousness; we have to sacrifice our past behaviour in order to be born again to our spiritual self. Only by our own will, desire and mastery of truth, can we really understand this. It is beyond an intellectual understanding, although intellectual 'know it all's' will argue against it, and for their own limitations of mind.

The Seventh Seal

Would a Christ want to make love to you? Well, maybe if you were also a Christ and you both wanted to seed a generation of potentially immaculate, impeccable beings! Christ is God-woman or God-man. It is God flowing unencumbered through human flesh. One who has fully-realised the unlimited mind of God has purified the flesh that houses the living God.

The greatest temple that was ever built is the human body because therein do we find our holy covenant with God.

A Christ is obviously not a lustful, first seal entity. Their energy permanently sits in the crowning seventh seal and they would never lower it for just a chemical hit on their body. Indeed, they are not addicted emotionally to any experience. In other words, they have left the past behind and are no longer encumbered by their memories.

Relationships can be experienced on all levels of consciousness, but it always takes a long period of emotional fasting to shift one's focus from the lower energy centres of the human drama. What determines the nature of the sexual relationship

The Blue Window

is the conscious intent of the participants. The energy of the first three seals is polarised so you attract to you, your opposite. In other words, a victim will always attract a tyrant and both will swing back and forth as the relationship develops. From the fourth seal upwards, the energy is wholesome, so like attracts like - self reflects self. For instance, a truly loving being will attract a similar loving mate and a truthful being will only attract a liar if their truth also includes them being a victim. Think about that one.

As we discussed earlier, most men are no greater than their base seal experience, whereas most women start from a higher point on the evolutionary scale. Women are naturally third seal beings and are therefore closer to God than most men. This really flies in the face of religion. I am a man yet I am saying that most women are closer to God than most men are! However, the trouble with most women is - they don't know it. Instead of continuing upward to the fourth and fifth seals, they anchor down to meet the men on the first rung of Jacob's ladder. For men, that is sex, but for women, it is their need to survive and their misconception that that requires having a man in their life. This is one of the many reasons why very few women ever live their truth. They compromise their greatness by being needy, for an illusionary identity and because they have never really accepted their equality with men. Instead of being 'breathtakingly beautiful goddesses', they are clever, manipulative, seductresses.

There can be a blending of the different frequencies of consciousness and energy across the whole light spectrum, but in the main, close human relationships are founded upon sex. If you were to ask most young couples to abstain from any physical contact for just two months, it would have a dramatic and detrimental effect upon most of their relationships. It's almost as if the sexual act itself confirms the relationship and without it, the emotional tie is broken. The man gets to feel like a man and the woman gets to feel like a woman and without that 'feeling', what else does the relationship have to offer? Is it really any surprise that most relationships which start out as just lust, don't work out?

In summarising this chapter, I would have to say that 99% of human relationships are founded upon emotional need. You may say 'so what?' And I will say, 'it is the emotion that is killing you'. You may say, 'I'd rather die happy than give up the life I know'. And I say, 'if that is your idea of happiness then go right ahead but you'll never know any more than you currently know'.

If you think you can't give up certain aspects of your life then that is your emotions talking to you, and evidence of your addiction to them. Just because I talk like this doesn't mean to say that I have mastered my emotions! Knowing a philosophical truth is one thing but living it is quite another matter! I am simply passing on what I know, for you to do with it whatever you want.

The Blue Window

Giving up the sources of your unhappiness is a difficult thing to do because it means the death of your self-created identities.

For most men, their emotional addictions are to sex, power, competition and taking from other men. The affairs of the competitive and powerful man are normally an extension of his career life. As long as 'her indoors' plays the role of 'slave' and caters for his every need; he will strive to give her just enough time to 'keep her sweet', and hopefully stop her from playing away from home. His time is divided something like 10% for the wife and family, 10% for all mistresses and 80% for his illusionary business life.

The powerful men are all about control, manipulation and the mental conditioning of their subjects. That is their idea of power. But in fact, power can either be used righteously or unrighteously. The higher, righteous use of power is only found in unconditional love. One only gets to know this higher power when one lets go of the *raw* power of the third seal.

The competitive man is running an old programme. Competition is a primeval warring instinct. Competitive sports people exemplify this truth. The competitive man not only competes on the sports field or in the boardroom; they compete with everyone they meet: including their mistresses, their wives and even their children!

Jealousy and war were originally born from competitive gods trying to outdo each other's creations. The bedding of another man's wife could also be seen in this vein. The illusionary pleasure of taking from another man, what he thinks belongs to him, is one-upmanship. The predator is robbed of energy and his actions cause another lesson for his soul to learn. This also applies to the competitive woman.

The sexual addict is normally also a predator. I know this animal well because I used to be one. You can get away with it when you are young, but once you get to middle age, you are on the slippery downward slope. If the emotion has got a hold on you and you're already past your prime, then it's going to take an incredible strength of will to avoid certain death. If you don't ride and tame the wild stallion before middle age, then you'll end up a happy 'gonna'! The inability of one to tame the stallion means one's days are numbered and lived only to feed one's emotional addictions.

So why do women acquiesce to the emotional needs of men? It should now be obvious that it is because of their emotional needs. Notwithstanding the fact that some women like the identity of being on the arm of a handsome or rich man, they have the misconception that somehow their security, indeed their survival, lies in the hands of us men. They are not naturally sexual beings and certainly

The Blue Window

not twice a day, every day, like some women brag about! So what are the real motives of women who engage in regular sex, if they are not addicted to the sex itself?

I have a friend who has said of her sex life with her husband, 'I enjoy it but I'm not really bothered'. Does that sound familiar to you? Why do you bother then? That is the question you women should answer honestly. If you haven't found the answer in the above, then you're going to need to do some deeper thinking...

When women can understand their emotional needs, look at them objectively, reveal the lies and be brave enough to pull the plug on them; they can move beyond their self-made prisons. If your man says to you, 'you don't need me anymore', then tell him the truth, 'no I don't!' And when you're fed up with being his slave, then send him packing. That is living your truth! If he is not 'good company' to be with then why are you with him? Get the wisdom from your current and past situations, let go and move on up to the 4th rung on Jacob's evolutionary ladder.

There is nothing wrong with knowing that your relationship is nothing more than both of you feeding each other's emotional needs. My God, that is what you are here to experience - the consciousness of the first three seals. But when is the time that there is no more wisdom to be had and where do you go from there? You can keep changing the scenery, bringing in new unconscious actors, but eventually you will get bored because you now have a greater knowledge that is waiting for you to experience. This knowledge doesn't necessarily mean the end of your existing relationship, because you and your partner can move to the fourth and fifth heavens together; providing both of you are willing to accept change.

When do we reach a point in our spiritual growth to where the source of our unhappiness becomes our gender? The illusionary identities of being a woman and being a man mean that we are under a self-imposed pressure to be that way. But in truth, are we not gods with no gender? If we are to live our truth, then eventually we have to do away with all the sources of stress and unhappiness. And ultimately that means moving our minds to where we no longer think of ourselves as men or women but instead we think as the gods we are.

So why do we bother with sex and relationships? Good question don't you think? If you're in a relationship, do you know the real reason why you're in it? And if so, is it a legitimate reason?

It seems to me that we're almost compelled to seek a partner in life so that we can be socially acceptable and so-called 'normal'. So what are the legitimate reasons for being in an intimate relationship? Are there really any legitimate

The Blue Window

reasons apart from bringing forth offspring?

Is a control drama a legitimate reason? Is financial dependence or support a legitimate reason? Is emotional dependence or support a legitimate reason? I'm just trying to get you to think here, so as to help you to expand your mind.

Personally, apart from procreation, I have found only 2 reasons to be so intimate with another person, and they are the company that results from 'minds in common' and the desire for sex. Leaving aside 'falling in love' because you're only really falling in love with your own ideal, and all the romance associated with that; can you think of any other reason? It's like Ramtha has said, "are you really in love with the person you're with or are you habitually creating a person in your life to meet some compromise in your mind?"

If your relationship is stressing you out, then please just realise where you are compromising your truth and firstly remedy that. I have found that when body-consciousness meets body-consciousness then the novelty soon wears off and both are on the slippery downward slope almost from the outset. That is why I put in my article entitled *Two people who love each other*, how important it is to be 'mindful' in your relationships. If it's not loving and joyful, what's the point?

Is it any wonder that masterful beings mainly walk alone, when you consider there are so few of them? And to entertain an idiot in their lives 'just for sex' would be both a compromise to their truth and really stupid. I have come to realise that our continuing advancement on our spiritual journeys is not about giving anything up, but rather 'living our truth without duality' automatically carves away at the past and certain experiences naturally fall away.

The really advanced man or woman invariably 'walks alone', unless they find their equal (in mind); in which case we then have a marriage made in Heaven (a soul union). The unenlightened will continue to seek (or remain with) a partner who mirrors what they unconsciously perceive they lack in themselves. O compromise, compromise, compromise (stress, stress, stress)!

Contribution by Mike Wright of RSE:

I have double checked the archives and spoken with Jaime, our editor in JZK Publishing. We both agree that Ramtha has consistently described women as nearer to god than men because men live primarily in the first seal and women live primarily in the *second* seal.

Reason it this way: The first seal is the power of brute survival of the fittest and the power to create a child. One can live an entire incarnation only responding

The Blue Window

emotionally to the stimulus of the environment and playing out the genetic program without any real conscious/contemplative/creative thoughts.

The second seal is social consciousness - family, children, parenting, group, club, membership, belonging, nation, creed, etc. It is here that women excel - the nurturer that surrenders the personal gain of the first seal life for the sake of the social group. It takes a village to raise a child...

The third seal is the power of control - those who rule, those who create everything the consumers consume, those who tell everyone what to think and why; what to do and when, those who give the masses the 'new and improved' product every season. These are the corporate leaders, the politicians, the military commanders, the priests and the pope.

Women are the slaves and servants and toys of powerful men. There are very few women in the ranks of power on planet earth these days. Powerful women were hunted down by the church centuries ago, because once women find their power, they are not dependent upon men any more.

Here is a quote from Ramtha: "Women are nearer to God. And once they find their own power, they need not men to be lovers anymore, which is men's greatest fear, because even if men fantasise about other men sexually, they still need the slave, the servant, the appearance, the affection, the forgiveness, the drama, and the tragedy. Women always provide men those opportunities, whereas men never do".

Note that Ramtha says, "once they find their own power". So women have the opportunity to move up from the second seal to the third but they will face the adversity of powerful men if they do. JZ is an example of just that.

Thanks for that Mike!

The Blue Window

ATTITUDE IS EVERYTHING

"Ah, well, let me tell you how people who do not possess the truth of the experience take scraps of it, pure truth, and like clear water they run it through the dirty rag of their consciousness and out comes muddy water. How many of you can see that visually?" – Ramtha

You are not what you eat; you are the result of your thinking. There are still a lot of people who think diet is the answer to almost every human ailment. That of course is their truth but it is a limited truth. As I have said in the chapter on Truth - there is truth in everything. Let us take a look at a hypothetical situation to try and illustrate the above point.

We have identical twins who go to see a dietician in an effort to improve their health. The one of them is reluctant but her sister drags her along. Both twins are the same height, weight, body-type and constitution. Their metabolic rates, lifestyles and existing diets are also identical. There is only one difference that separates them - their attitudes.

The dietician naturally recommends the same change in diet for both. The reluctant one reluctantly agrees to give it a try for three months and the other one is happy to incorporate the changes into her lifestyle; because she instinctively knows it is right for her.

The reluctant one has a pessimistic attitude. She thinks these super foods are all a load of hype, and she's determined to prove her sister wrong. Further, she's the type who is inclined to look at life through the eyes of judgement. Everything is black and white to her and everybody is either right or wrong, good or bad or positive and negative. You know the type? She typically criticises and ridicules other people.

Her sister, on the other hand, is very much the opposite. She is optimistic about the future. She looks at life through loving eyes and understands and loves her sister. Her only motive is to help them both. She also realises that first and foremost she must love herself and take complete responsibility for her own health. And part of that love of self is to love her body by feeding it with nutritious, super foods. Her world is full of dreams of happiness and perfect health. Her partner is supportive and they plan to live a very long life together, by staying in pristine condition. When she looks at other people she always sees the best in them.

The three months have passed and both women have stuck to the regime impeccably. To the one, it was a diet that she was glad to see the back of, and she still has her list of ailments to prove her sister wrong! To the other, it became a

The Blue Window

new way of eating, which she enjoyed so much that she forgot about her ailments. Her pristine health continues to reflect her beautiful attitude.

Our own attitudes are the precursors of everything that we do in life. We seem to have an attitude about everything. Indeed,

"Attitude is everything" - Ramtha.

You can have an excellent diet but if you have a foul attitude you won't enjoy excellent health. The truth is, your diet will reflect your attitude about yourself. If there is a lack of self-love then you are more likely to abuse your body. Go and take another look in the mirror. What is your body trying to tell you about your state of mind? If you are overweight and/or not in perfect health, then ask yourself these questions,

1 Am I a liar or a cheat (the white ones count too)?
2 Do I live and speak my truth?
3 Am I lazy?
4 Am I greedy?
5 Am I a taker?
6 When I give is it truly unconditional?
7 Is my life just one big compromise?
8 Do I fear letting go and therefore don't let go?
9 Do I always see the best in other people?
10 Do I love unconditionally or do I judge others?
11 Do I like the attention my illness brings me?
12 Do I blame other people for aspects of my life?
13 Is there anything I hate?
14 Do I have any anger in me?

Your body has no choice - it automatically follows your mind. Only you can change the way that you think. And your every thought counts. If your mind is uneasy then your body will become diseased and age quickly. However, if your mind is tranquil then you will have a body that is harmonious with it, and you will be closer to becoming ageless.

I am no longer amazed at the vast amount of people who think that their aches and pains are the result of ageing, as if ageing was some sort of dreaded disease. Your body will not fail you as a result of the clock ticking away but rather it is your mind that believes this commonly agreed upon reality. You look at other people and you see what appears to be the ravishes of time and you just assume that is how it is. But what if the commonality that is creating the observed reality is the way you all think? Your thinking creates your reality.

The Blue Window

Take a look around you and observe other people as well as yourself. Everybody is sporting a different array of attitudes, coming from their genetics and their social conditioning. These attitudes are emotional programmes that chemically block the receptor sites of otherwise healthy body cells. It does not matter how 'good' your diet is, if there is no room for its nutritional uptake into your cells. If your body is not 'taking up' the nutrients it needs because of your attitudes, then you're going to be constantly hungry, no matter how much you eat. Being greedy, mean and not letting go, are all attitudes.

I remember going to a Ramtha event and Ramtha gave us this great teaching on the quantum world. Towards the end of the teaching he was talking about how we are all literally swimming in an unfathomable intelligence, which is constantly trying to press unlimited mind to us; but it is our limiting attitudes that are preventing our receivership of this higher consciousness. Earlier at the same event he had shown me my arrogance and consequently I could see how this attitude had thwarted my personal growth towards enlightenment. What attitudes do you have and what are you not willing to see or listen to because of them?

You're limiting attitudes are what closes down your mind and thus are what also causes you to age.

Many years ago I had a relationship with a woman for seven years. Unfortunately, never the minds would meet, successfully. Early on in the relationship I found myself out of work with plenty of time on my hands. My partner, on the other hand, was extremely busy with her work, often working twelve-hour days. It was wintertime and I was picking up just about every bug going around. Yet she was incredibly healthy at the time. I said to her, 'how come you never get sick?' She said, 'I don't have time to be sick'. I've since realised what a powerful statement that is. Let us take a look at why this is:

You cannot speak anything from your mouth that is not the conclusion of your conscious thought processes. Everything you speak is the conclusion of your conscious mind and if it includes the word 'I' then it is empowered by your subconscious mind and becomes absolute law in your reality. The conscious and subconscious minds kind of line up and marry when the word 'I' is used. So we should be very careful what we earnestly say about ourselves, especially if we believe it and mean it.

'I don't have time to be sick'. This was my partner's truth; there was no doubt in her conscious mind. The statement automatically lined up with her subconscious mind because it contained the right language and that was her reality - she was never sick. As I mentioned in an earlier chapter, every reality is created and it can only exist in time. Therefore a reality cannot exist if there is 'no time' for it.

The Blue Window

THE BOX

We are all like a 'Jack in the box'. Our box is our self-imposed prison of illusion. We share our box with everything and everyone from our past. It is a box that is held together by our own lacks, needs, fears, superstitions, dogmas, beliefs, greed, judgements, impatience, intolerance, unresolved emotions, limiting attitudes; and so on. And the other people in our box reflect back to us our own lack or strength, otherwise they wouldn't be there with us.

You can only see in another person what exists in you. If it didn't exist in you, you wouldn't be able to recognise it in them. So what you see in them is a mirror to you. What is your mirror trying to tell you about you? Do you have a lack that is in common with another person in your life? Or are they mirroring to you a quality you have yet to own in yourself? When you understand why you need other people in your life, it is then a matter of owning that lack and eventually retiring those needs.

Let us take a quick look at a common problem and misconception coming from our own ignorance. Your parents live 10 minutes up the road, your brother or sister lives 10 minutes down the road and you work just around the corner. Give or take a few miles, is this close to your picture? If so, you're stuck in your box. Believe it or not, your own thoughts towards your family, cage your spirit. You can only fly free when you let go emotionally.

Please try to understand that in the greater scheme of things, we are all brothers and sisters in one huge family. The only reason we were born to our parents is we shared a commonality with them, on a soul level; that needed to be worked out and healed. There are a few who have been very fortunate. Their parents have been their greatest teachers. But for most people, they never realise why they are born to their parents until they pass from this world and undergo yet another light review.

This area of family is most graphically shown on the excellent film 'What Dreams May Come' with Robin Williams. When you truly understand reincarnation you will accept that your grandchildren could also be your deceased parents or grandparents. Or you could be your parent's or grandparent's deceased parent, obviously if they died before you were born. Give this matter some thought; it will expand your mind.

Your Box is your self-imposed prison of limited thinking. When you start to expand your mind you will pop out of your Box and start to view life through a new window; just to retract again like Jack! It takes a very brave person to let go of the past completely. The past is comfortable; it's where all of your old identities

The Blue Window

are. Who might you be without them?

If we draw a small rectangle on a piece of paper and write the words 'Subjective Mind' in it, then everything outside of the box would represent 'Objective Mind'. We only use about 5% of our brain's capacity to perpetuate our subjective realities, so the other 95% is obviously for a more expansive, objective viewpoint!

Another example of your box is boredom. It means it's time for you to have a new experience instead of keep repeating the same old stuff of the past. If your life is basically always the same, if it is predictable, then is it any wonder that you are bored? An interesting person isn't going to stick around for too long because you don't bring anything to the table.

"Boredom is a sign from the soul that you have learned everything there is to learn in that adventure". - Ramtha

This world is a mirrored consciousness; you should always look at your life and ask, 'what is it trying to tell me about me?' Eventually, we learn that the mirror is actually a grand illusion, and is only there for the purpose of knowing ourselves through self-reflection. The greater truth is what lies behind the mirror. Our bodies are simply recognition of who we were and not who we are. When we shift our focus and start to strive to be a mind, then we are striving for something that does not have gender and therein lies our greatness. We should never identify ourselves with our bodies; otherwise we are doomed to being no greater than the clay itself. And we are not the clay, we are the moulders of it!

If your life is just about how you look, what a great body you've got, what you are wearing, who you are sleeping with or what you are having for dinner tonight; then you're going to be extremely boring to anyone who is intelligent. You might look great but how long is that going to last?

All it takes is a shift of focus to alleviate boredom and to cultivate a greater mind. We will never find great mind in mediocrity. Fleeting moments of entertainment may temporarily alleviate boredom but a permanent solution lies in the constant acquisition of new knowledge. Knowledge and the courage to change are keys to our inner universe.

My experience has taught me that without knowledge we are lost in the wilderness and doomed to experience yet another carnal existence, after this one. We accept death as a part of life and this is obviously fatal. We can never become immortal if we accept our own death. However, when we accept new knowledge, we are automatically creating a future time-line, to be experienced at some time in the future. Acceptance is the key to programming the soul.

The Blue Window

COME DIVE WITH ME

Many years ago I took up the rather expensive sport of scuba diving. After completing the initial basic training and open-water dives, in a local submerged quarry, I then invested in the best diving suit and equipment I could buy. I realised that my adventures underwater weren't without risk, so only the best equipment would do. After thirty or so cold water dives in poor visibility, I decided to try some clear warm water and booked a holiday to Menorca with my partner.

The first day's diving was fantastic; it exceeded all of my expectations. On the second day, I'd got a bit of a cold and was congested in the nose but didn't think too much of it, as I was focused on the dive ahead and keen to experience another interlude in the ocean.

We all entered the water and the whole party seemed to descend rather quickly, my diving buddy leaving me behind. In my efforts to catch up, I continued to descend even though I had experienced pain in my right ear at a depth of about 5 metres. I caught up with my buddy at 18 metres but by this time I was dizzy and nauseated. I knew that they intended to go deeper and although I wanted to follow, my condition was deteriorating rapidly and I was concerned about maintaining consciousness. I attracted the attention of my buddy with those funny hand signals and we made a normal controlled ascent to the surface.

At the surface, my buddy fully inflated my jacket and I removed the regulator from my mouth and started to spit blood. It flashed through my mind that my Mother had had a brain haemorrhage at the same age and I wondered if the same had happened to me! To cut a long story short, I ended up in hospital and it was 4 days before I could stand unaided and 4 months before the vertigo left me. It was an interesting experience to say the least! Fortunately, I had only ruptured the membranes of my middle ear and the blood had found its way down into my throat. I had survived another close encounter with death.

At one of my RSE events, Ramtha described how the experience of diving can be likened to life itself. The diving suit is the body you wear and the sensory gauges represent the body's senses and involuntary movements. You are obviously going to choose the most appropriate body and equipment for your planned adventure, to make known the unknown. Isn't that the purpose of diving - to explore the unknown depths looking for hidden treasure?

You've done your intricate planning, you know the souls in your party and you have pre-planned the meeting places and times with your brothers and sisters. You've checked your body suit and gauges and you know your tanks are filled with enough spiritual will to get you back to the surface. Your brothers and sisters

The Blue Window

all have the same ultimate agenda, although their chosen paths are very different, because you are all looking to fill your diving bags with a different array of treasures. You know you will cross paths with them at the planned times and places because these meetings offer you the pearls of wisdom you are lacking to complete your mission in the dark, deep depths of the ocean.

You all do your final checks and you jump! As you descend, the pressure increases and the light starts to dim and you finally lose each other in the dark, murky depths. All you have is a map drawn on a slate board, a torch and a compass. Needless to say, some of the party lose their way and run out of spiritual will. You are one of the best treasure hunters because you trust in your intuition instead of focusing upon how your body suit feels or what your gauges read.

You meet up with some of your expedition along the way and you start to identify with them by body suit and equipment because that is all you can see. Furthermore, you start to identify yourself with your body suit and its gauges. This is when you stop being intuitive and become more concerned by how you are feeling. Consequently, you lose your way, ending up going around in circles, only to come back to the same old places of the past.

The diving is fun at times and at other times it is frightening. The fear of the unknown and the fear of death are what keeps you focused upon your body suit and its gauges. You take solace in the fact you keep meeting up with the same old 'body suits' and you reason that this is just the way diving is. Although you know your spiritual energy is running out, you have changed from being the diver in control of the suit to being the suit itself, and thus you have forgotten when you jumped into the water and descended into the dense, slow world of the bottom of the sea. Moreover, you have forgotten your original agenda - to return to the surface with a full bag! And you've even forgotten that you're on a treasure hunt, hunting for pearls of wisdom!

My personal diving experience taught me that it was my choice not to go any deeper and that had probably saved my life. Just imagine if I had died and popped out of my body suit. The 'lords of the light' would have said to me, 'to get back to the surface you must first return to the deep dark depths, to complete your diving expedition and become heavily laden with treasure. Then and only then will you know how to ascend'.

The problem with humanity is we think we are the diving suits who are trying to be the divers, not realising and accepting that we really are the divers who have chosen to wear the diving suits, to experience certain things that can only be experienced whilst wearing the suits. Said another way, we really are spiritual beings who are wearing our bodies as vehicles of expression here.

The Blue Window

HUMAN POTENTIAL

This chapter is going to be mainly about the vast untapped potential of the human brain, because therein lies our potential to receive a higher consciousness, to create a greater mind and thus create a reality consistent with the depth of that mind. For instance, an objective mind realises far greater potentials and creates far greater realities than a mind that looks at the world subjectively.

Ramtha has taught that the brain is a multidimensional, quantum, bio-computer, which can house unlimited potentials coming from the mind of God.

The subconscious part of your brain, found in your lower cerebellum, houses the whole of the mind of God albeit subconsciously. If something in you remains subconscious then you are always going to be none the wiser. It is only when you start to wake it up and become conscious of it, do you realise there is a part of you that is both awesome and sublime.

We associate with everything and everyone in our life, for the survival of our physical and emotional bodies (by way of our bodily senses); yet there is obviously vast untapped potentials that exist outside of the boxes of our limited realities, just sitting there waiting for us to experience.

We equate the past with being real, yet the brain doesn't know what is real or not! If we imagine something, our brain cannot tell whether it is real in the terms of how we perceive what is real. Reality to the brain is what is imaged and held in the frontal lobe. So if we create an ideal of how we want to be, then there is nothing to stop us from simply being it, providing we hold that focus and don't carve it up with the swords of fear and doubt. Our lofty thoughts have to become our common thinking. In other words, we have to build bigger models of thought to experience the untapped potentials that lie dormant in us.

If we create reality by what we focus upon and if the brain cannot distinguish between what is real or not, then if we focus consistently upon our dreams instead of our addictive environment, eventually we will experience the miraculous instead of the mundane and ordinary. It is a matter of whether we want to be ordinary or extraordinary?

It is our attitudes that shape our brain's neurological network and this produces the peptides in our brains that are directly proportional to the number of receptor sites in our cells. The numbers of receptor sites are directly proportional to our expression of DNA and thus our expression of life. It is our expression of life that determines our state of health. So, following that through, we see clearly that our attitudes affect our state of health. (My thanks to Dr Bruce Lipton for this).

The Blue Window

If we add to the above equation the fact that we only use about 3% of our DNA for physical expression (the other 97% lies dormant in us and is regarded as 'junk' DNA), then we see why our reality is so small and our health so impaired. A small knowledge base equals a small reality and fragile health, whereas a large knowledge base brings a greater reality and excellent health. It is new knowledge that feeds our cells and rejuvenates them. And it is a lack of knowledge (evidenced by our emotional addictions) that kills cells and eventually kills our bodies. We either rejuvenate our cells with knowledge or degenerate them without it.

Perhaps you don't want to listen because you think you are superior in your knowledge but you are just another 'know it all'. You deny anything that doesn't fit in your little box of reality, because you're image feels it may get shattered, and it will. You are quick to anger and blame other people for your complacent attitudes. Your know what the real problem is, but you are too much of a coward to do anything about it. You lost your courage in compromise, doubt and guilt. You fear getting old yet you won't embrace change in your life, so growing old and dying is a certainty, if you have fears. You look outside of yourself to run down and criticise other people, because this deflects attention away from the real problem - you and your inability to face yourself. And you wonder why you are not in perfect health!

While all this is going on, the observer in you just watches and loves you through your ignorance and wonders when you're going to wake up and stop acting so immaturely? You may well be an adult in terms of your physical appearance and your earthly years but how grown up are you really, in terms of the whole of cosmic consciousness? God you may well be but if you act like an infantile then you are not the example of God expressing fully in a woman or a man, which you could be.

Your spiritual journey is like walking blindfold through an enclosed labyrinth; every wall of the labyrinth that you bump into offers you a choice of direction to go in. Your choices determine how quickly you find the centre or if you find it at all. You can be as close as your breath, yet if you choose your past feelings instead of your instinctual knowingness, then you keep coming back to the same old places of the past.

Said another way, you are swimming in a sea of emotion, bathing in those 'good feelings'; unaware of the distant shore that offers you a new life. The distant shore is wild, outrageous, bizarre, bountiful, exotic and an exquisite place. It is a mysterious, enchanting forest of unlimited new knowledge; that does not beckon you but is always there for you when you get tired of bathing in the chemical sea. Bathing in this sea is the ever-present temptation. Do you ever make it to the distant shore?

The Blue Window

DEMONS AND JUDGEMENT

Where do I start with this chapter? I have chosen to address this subject because it affects all of us. Firstly, perhaps I should try to explain what demons are and what judgement is, because I know they are misunderstood terms.

We are quick to judge and to get angry. Alongside doubt they are probably our greatest flaws. They are evidence of the animal in us. Only last night, I heard on the news how a couple had adopted a 4-year-old boy and over a period of time they had subjected him to the most horrendous physical abuse, culminating in them biting him and bludgeoning him to death. They both got just 8 years! And I, like many of you, was sitting there with visions of literally kicking their heads in. I can't say that I was angry because this kind of occurrence is all to frequent these days, but I was quick to judge them and exact my own punishment on behalf of the innocent boy. Apparently, he was a happy boy until they adopted him.

Later that evening I realised the flaw in my own personality. How am I to know the 'unfinished business' of a little god in a 4-year-old boy's body? Maybe he was Hitler in his last life (assuming Hitler is dead!) and this event was necessary to balance his karma? The chance of the boy being an incarnation of Adolf is, of course, more remote than winning the national lottery; but when you understand what I am saying here, you will understand reincarnation. Human consciousness is not currently sufficiently evolved enough to know the unresolved emotion of another soul, and thus we are quick to anger and to judge others. This is evidence of the ignorance of our race.

A society cannot exist in harmony without some sort of correctional programme for crime offenders, but we should also understand that we become the effects of our own actions through successive lives. We are not really accountable to other men and women but we are accountable to our parent, God. Not that God has ever judged us! It is simply that our thoughts and actions determine our future days and this 'quantum fact' doesn't die with the death of our physical bodies...

Let us look at another example. The current war in Afghanistan. The Americans have just started their ground offensive after a relentless campaign of bombing strategist targets and the odd hospital and refugee bus. What have they achieved thus far? The killing of innocent civilians and a humanitarian crisis that doesn't bear thinking about! All of this has been done, so they say, as part of the fight against terrorism. What about the terror they are instilling in those poor, innocent, Afghan people? It's one thing throwing out a few million dollars worth of aid for propaganda purposes but what about the billions of dollars worth of damage they are causing? Why are they really doing it and who is going to pick up the tab? Could it really be because of the oil pipeline that the oil barons want to run from

The Blue Window

Uzbekistan through Turkmenistan and Afghanistan to the coast of Pakistan; thus avoiding buying oil from the Arabs? No doubt we are eventually going to see another country controlled by the World Bank and its lending arms. Could that be the American's ulterior motive? Only time will reveal the truth.

Here is another example of judgement. This month we have seen another paedophile and murderer imprisoned at our expense. Why are we supporting these people who are obviously a nuisance to our society? After all is said and done, we are not responsible for them. If they want to create their own hell on earth, then let's give it to them! Let's ship them to some remote, desolate island and give them some basic tools and seeds to plant. And nothing more. If they choose to spend their time buggering themselves to death, then let them do it to each other, away from our precious children. It's time we got tough with these people. It's the only way we're going to rid our society of their menace. The trouble is, there are too many people in authority in our country who are also paedophiles. Let us put all these animals together, pen them in and let them fight for their lives. No more luxury stays in open prisons; just basic survival. That will soon change their focus and cause them to think differently.

The above paragraph is coming from my lower mind, the judgmental animal in me that wants to see harsh punishment for such crimes. The perspective coming from the fourth seal and above would seek to harmonise our world by providing institutionalised, correctional, behavioural programmes for such individuals, even if it means disabling those beyond help, so they are rendered harmless to our society. Any offenders who successfully reform their personalities should be welcomed back into society by open, loving arms.

Why do you think we keep spinning our wheels and repeating the same old experiences of the past? It is because we keep laying our judgements on our experiences. This applies individually and in whole societies. Why do the Israeli's and the Palestinians keep fighting? Because they keep judging one another. Judgement is not love; it is the antithesis of love.

When Jesus the Christ said, 'follow me', he meant for us to become non-judgmental and to love our neighbours as if they were ourselves; and indeed they are. Let us all start to treat other people as we would want to be treated. And let us stop pointing the finger at others but rather show them, by example, the way forward with love.

I have learned from Ramtha that when people die and go to the light they undergo a 'Light Review'. What do you think they see? They see the effect of their own judgements. That is why some religions call it 'Judgement Day'. It's not that God judges you. God is incapable of doing that. What loves unconditionally cannot

The Blue Window

judge. The two states are just not compatible. For more detail about this listen to the Ramtha CDs 'The Planes of Bliss'.

What Ramtha tells us is that all seven levels of consciousness exist simultaneously in the same moment, and that all times and space exist now. This also means that all lifetimes exist simultaneously in the now moment. So who we are now is the product of our many lifetimes and all those lifetimes exist in us now. We are the greatest we have ever been, now. So, are we not viewing our life 'in the light' right now? And are we not living our 'light review' now?

Quantum Mechanics tells us that all of our potentials exist now and therefore whatever we think at any and all times, is the truth. If the Kingdom of Heaven is within us, and it is, then we are the truth, because we are creating reality every moment of every day from the thoughts we entertain. *We are both the creators and the truth.* This is what religion doesn't want us to know and what science has yet to fully understand and appreciate.

Please take your time with this book. It has taken me many years to know what I know. To sit for hours and contemplate on the above paragraph alone will greatly expand your mind. *Be patient with yourself.*

If we are living our light reviews now, and according to Ramtha we are, then it would be wise if we changed from being judgmental people to loving people.

Please remember that you are a multidimensional being and although you may not be conscious yet of the so-called higher aspects of yourself; your every thought is creating your reality now and into the future. Your every thought counts and it affects your potentials on every level. It goes straight up the line. Whatsoever you think determines your actions and the effects are what you reap, transcendent of whether you remain a mortal being or become immortal.

When we understand the above it engenders in us a sense of responsibility for how we think and what we choose to create. We can no longer blame other people for our lives and must finally take full responsibility for ourselves. God doesn't care what we create; it is the source of our creations; indeed, it is the energy that everything has been created from.

It should now be plain and obvious to you. If you want to create a beautiful future for yourself, and live in a world that is loving, that is at peace and knows truth; then you have got to become responsible for your thinking and what you allow to manifest in your life. It is no longer tenable that you have a victim or tyrannical consciousness. That kind of consciousness does not bring peace, harmony or freedom. Moving to a non-judgmental state of being is a very advanced, objective

The Blue Window

state of mind. It is the state of mind of advanced civilisations that do live in peace, harmony and true freedom.

Before I move completely away from judgement, I want to talk with you about self-judgement and guilt. They are really one and the same thing. Guilt is wishing we knew then what we now know. This is particularly relevant when we come into new knowledge and then we look back at our pasts and judge ourselves in the light of the new knowledge. As I said earlier, both innocence and ignorance are entirely forgivable, and how could we possibly have known then what we now know? We may indeed look back and be somewhat ashamed at some of our past actions but to judge ourselves for those actions is a foolish thing to do.

So why is it, even when we know the above, do we still judge ourselves and feel guilty? It is because we have become addicted to the feeling of being guilty. *Emotional addiction is what separates us from greatness.*

If wisdom is garnered through experience, and it is, what have we got to be ashamed of? We want to come to a place in our mind where we say out loud, 'I forgive myself for my past, those memories that stick out in my mind. I let go of my past and forget it. My past is no longer a part of me. I am healed and made a new person. I come to the river in my mind, I bath in the river and the holy water washes away my past. I am no longer my past. It is no more. I walk to the other side of the river. I don't look back. I leave no footprints in the past. I am the first of my generation to reach the other side. Many more will follow me. I am the anointed one. My God blesses me and my Holy Spirit descends upon me. I am born again to a new life to where I follow the true teachings of all masters who have passed this way before me. I have been baptised and I look forward to a transpersonal reality.'

In my life I can now see how I have lied for the sake of my own good feelings. I have been insincere, untrustworthy, disingenuous, dishonourable, a taker and a conman. I have used and manipulated other people for the continuity of my emotional feelings. My body and its chemicals have always justified their needs. I have used, abused and hurt people for the sake of my own selfish emotional addictions. It's not that I ever intended to use or hurt people. It's simply that I was blinded by the light.

When we move to the other side, we realise that our past behaviour was just a part of being human and it was righteous for us to experience it and then move on. How else can we master our humanity if not through the experience of it?

If we had done what we were supposed to do, we would have created an experience, then moved in to emotionally embrace it, captured its wisdom, and

The Blue Window

then moved on to the next experience (source: Ramtha).

Every physical experience is also an emotional experience. As the environment stimulates the body's senses, the neuro-peptides are released into the bloodstream. The body is now looking for satisfaction, 'that' feeling that it knows only too well. A good example is sex. Almost any aspect of our environment can arouse us sexually. It may just be our mind's association with a colour! If we allow that arousal to germinate, then the known outcome is the orgasm that redeems the stress the body is under. The trouble is, it becomes a viscous circle, in that we are then chemically addicted to the orgasm for satisfaction; and because it feels so good, we know exactly how to stimulate the body to complete the cycle. Our sexual addiction is one of the many emotional addictions that are causing our bodies to age prematurely and eventually to die.

I think it is now fitting that I write about demons and what they are. A demon is a construct of your mind that compels you to experience an emotional addiction. Probably the easiest way to explain this is to ask you to think about what you think about when you masturbate. Well, obviously it varies a lot but you will find that it is either a fantasy or a memory. The demons are the fantasies and the phantoms are the memories you like to replay. They both serve the same purpose and they are both just as easy to call up or create. In the context of masturbation, your demons are the firing of created holographic images that arouse you for the desired feeling and its climax. They are your secret moments that you think nobody knows about. Your phantoms are usually the re-enactment of memories of your favourite lovers who you can screw time and time again. A phantom can also be moulded into a demon, if you fancy spicing up your memory a bit! Let's be honest here, you can lay anything on another person for the sake of your chemical fix.

The reason I'm using masturbation as an example, is because it's one of those taboo subjects that nobody wants to talk about, nobody likes to admit to it, yet everybody does it. Unless you intend to follow through on your demons and make them a reality, what does the act of masturbation mean in the presence of your own mind constructs? All it means is you are screwing your demons!

How then do we reconcile telling the truth with the above knowledge? The next time we have a conversation with the neighbour, do we look them in the eye and tell them that they gave us a helping hand last night? Do we ring up our previous partner and tell them that it is they who still blow our little cotton socks off? And when we're having sex with the monkey, do we tell him it's really Tom Jones who's doing the business for us? These are valid questions where living a lie is concerned. Equally, demons not only apply to sexual activity; they are commonplace in distorting reality: to feed all fear-based emotions.

The Blue Window

These creatures of our minds are like a wild fire out of control. Each time we have an emotional experience it is as if we light a campfire in a vast forest. The redemption of the experience feels like we have put out the fire, but in fact, it is still smouldering, waiting to be rekindled. The forest represents the neurological network of our analytical brain and every now and then a fire starts and spreads out of control, in a part of the forest. The demons are alive and spreading in us and they will keep raging until they are satisfied. As soon as we put one fire out, it's as if another starts. The closer we get to the river the more the demons rage. We keep satisfying them but it's no good, they never go away completely and come back to plague us. There's no reprieve and no such thing as returning to being normal. We either live with them and continue to satisfy them or we chop their heads off by crossing the river. There is no fire on the other side of the river. Don't you ever doubt that!

The Blue Window

FAIRNESS AND EQUALITY

It seems fitting that I have arrived at writing this chapter at exactly the same time as the terrorist attack on America. My love and understanding goes out to all those who are struggling to come to terms with what has happened. This event exemplifies the world we now live in. What I am most interested in is why did it happen? Why do large populations of the world hate America so much?

It is obvious that it is because of what the American authorities stand for. That is not to say that I condone the actions of the terrorists, on the contrary, I deplore their actions. It is rather that I am seeking to understand what has caused this horrendous tragedy and unnecessary loss of human life.

You may be thinking 'what has this got to do with expanding individual consciousness and eventually changing global consciousness?' An advanced consciousness equates a more objective mindset; so to move in that direction we have to get out of our boxes and make an effort to understand national and global issues. Believe it or not, we are not separate from the world in which we live, and the 'stage directors' are influencing our world on a daily basis. If we don't like the conditions we are living under, then we need to become 'aware' of the truth and make a stand for that!

Osama Bin Laden calls America an 'Imperialist' state. Let us define what Imperialism is. My Webster's student dictionary says, 'a policy that aims at creating, maintaining, or extending an empire comprising other nations, territories etc., all controlled by a central government. The development or exploitation of the economic resources of another country without necessarily assuming direct political control'. Is Osama Bin Laden therefore correct? Is the now forming coalition, which includes some European countries, Russia, Pakistan, India, Israel and even China; evidence of America's imperialistic stance?

George Bush definitely appears to be in charge and Tony Blair has rushed across to be his right-hand man. Eradicating terrorism by non-peaceful means and getting the Middle-eastern countries to acquiesce, through monetary control, will leave a world under the indirect control of the US. Is that not the aim of the American government - to have centralised world control? Think about it. It was the One World Financial Centre that got blown up. Perhaps the terrorists can see the bigger picture and don't want to be controlled by Western financiers and their pseudo-democracies?

I do not think that terrorism is the new evil but rather it is a symptom of the ongoing evil - Capitalism. Please don't get me wrong here - I don't have a problem with people making a healthy profit from their entrepreneurial endeavours,

The Blue Window

providing they are not at the deliberate downfall of another person or concern. But it seems to me that we have cultivated a system here in the west where the rich are getting richer and the poor keep chasing the elusive dream. Where is the fairness and equality in our society?

Capitalism only works for the rich and the budding entrepreneurs amongst us. And even these new kids on the block seem to go only so far before they hit the unseen brick wall. It's almost as if the top seats only change hands amongst a select few. The poor are sold a dream and then mind-controlled into believing they are unworthy of attaining it. They are left with an inferiority complex believing that the rich are in some way superior to them.

Over the years a huge gulf has occurred in the standard of living of people in the west. Let me just give you a few examples of what has been broadcast in the U.K this year (2001):

Recently, in an effort to bring the public sector into line with the private sector, Tony Blair announced that the top civil servants would now earn around 200K a year. This means that some glorified secretaries can now earn £4000 per week! That's 4 times the turnover of my partners' business and she employs 6 staff! That's 14 times what I am currently earning and over 10 times what I will be earning if I qualify. It is also 10 times what a fire officer gets and they put their lives at increased risk every time the blue light goes on! Where is the fairness and equality in our society?

The Institute of Directors recently announced that the average pay of top executives is now 506K a year, yet the average pay of us workers is only around 23K. These top executives now earn on average 20 times more than the average worker. Do you not find that outrageous? Where is the fairness and equality in our society?

Earlier this year there was a lady who received a 500K bonus for helping to secure the lottery contract for Camelot. That is outrageous! Even a tenth of that amount is outrageous. A 5K bonus would have been more appropriate and yet still significant. I thought the lottery money was supposed to be for prize payouts and good causes? I have obviously been misinformed! Do you know that that is more money than most people in this country will ever accumulate? And she got it as a single bonus at our expense! Where is the fairness and equality in our society?

This year we have also seen Tony Blair receive a 47K pay rise and the boss of Railtrack got a 50K pay rise taking him to 450K a year. I don't know about you but I feel I'm worth more than 1/32nd of his salary; his pay rise alone is over 4 times my salary! The recent demise of the company Marconi didn't stop its Chief

The Blue Window

Executive from receiving 702K a year and renewing his one-year contract. And he was reportedly the cause of Marconi's demise! Where is the fairness and equality in our society?

The royal family swan around at the taxpayer's expense, appearing to do the correct thing, which is obviously very difficult for Philip and Edward. They earn huge sums of money, which they employ to further their own commercial interests. For God's sake, we have made the Queen the richest woman in the world. And she can't even write her own speeches! How long are we going to allow this pompous, ceremonial claptrap to continue?

The way we treat the royal family, anybody would think they are better or more valuable than you or I. I can tell you, in the eyes of God, they are no different to you and I; they are made of exactly the same stuff. And as for value, only ignorant people measure a person's value by how much income they bring in or by their bank balance. So why are we treating the royal family any different to how we would treat our other neighbours? Wake up people. The royal family have been parasites on the back of humanity for far too long. They receive a disproportionate income for the representative work they do. They should be stripped of their wealth and it given back to the people.

I could go on but I don't see the point. I hope you do. Suffice to say that Capitalism has created a very unfair and unequal monster of a society in the West. And look at the effects of Capitalism in Russia. The average Russian is worse off now than they were under Socialism. And I am not an advocate of Socialism either. It just breeds a society of powerless, irresponsible individuals. Is there a middle of the road answer? There must be.

Knowledge is the only possible answer to the problems we are experiencing. Jesus the Christ said, 'love your neighbour as you would love yourself'. He didn't say, 'love your neighbour only if they do as you tell um!' This means we should be giving unconditionally to our neighbours. How much can we give without conditions? Take a look at the situation in Palestine. Why don't we just give the Palestinians the land that was originally theirs, until Jehovah descended upon them? Just give it to them and live in peace. Be finished with the matter. But instead we have the American influence, which is obviously on the side of the Israelis, not wanting to relinquish any control. That's American imperialism at work. The Americans only get seriously interested in brokering peace deals when it suits their agenda...

I am an advocate of love and peace. True love is not expressed in an individual who desires control or a government that desires absolute control of our movements and resources.

The Blue Window

SOUL DESTINY OR MERRY-GO-ROUND

Now that you are conversant with the seven levels of consciousness, how they interact with your body through your body's energy centres, and how your brain facilitates consciousness to be experienced emotionally; the result of which is your mind: we can now determine the role of your soul and how your personality can reflect it or reflect what is known as your altered-ego.

Human consciousness is currently principally found in the polarised thinking of the first three seals. These lower realms of consciousness are collectively known as the altered-ego. Ego is what God is, in its highest form, but in its lowest form it becomes altered due to the splitting and polarisation of the energy that then carries an altered consciousness. We therefore see varying degrees of mental aberration occurring in human consciousness that does not occur in more advanced civilisations on the fourth and fifth dimensions.

Your personality is your individuality and it will always reflect how you have evolved consciously and where your energy is held. Take your sense of humour for instance. It could be witty and clean or it could be racist and crude. A sense of humour is a great gift but we can see how easy it is to poison it. In normal human consciousness, your personality will reflect your altered-ego for most of the time. There are times, however, when your personality will reflect your ego; those godly qualities you possess, such as being kind and caring towards another person. Those acts, if sincere and without ulterior motive, are certainly rewarded where it counts - in your soul.

So what is your soul? Simply put - it is your conscience (source: Ramtha).

In order to complete your chosen destiny, it is a matter of reforming your personality to reflect your innate, inborn, intuitive nature rather than the polarised thinking of your altered-ego.

It doesn't matter how we have lived our lives to date. What matters is whether we have gleaned the wisdom from our experiences and left those experiences behind. Far too many people are living in the past, yet the past really doesn't exist; it's just memories. However, many of us choose to live in those memories. What kind of ongoing life is that? We're backwards and going nowhere. We may as well be dead!

Life is to be lived in the moment. If we tie up the now moment in our memories, we miss out on those precious now moments. Let us let go of the past and move on, no matter how old our bodies are. We may have been the biggest scoundrel and rascal ever known but does that mean we cannot change our behaviour? We

The Blue Window

may have been miss goody two shoes but does that mean we cannot change and stop living a pretence?

Sooner or later we all have to clean up our acts. There is no place to hide and no place to go except within. We do not become a greater spiritual person by visiting Glastonbury or by going to live in Tibet or by sitting with some self-proclaimed guru in India. *We become greater through self-mastery.*

Every lesson we need to learn is staring us in the face right now. Our life and how we express it, is evidence of what we still have yet to own as wisdom. The trouble is, *we don't see our own flaws because we are them*, and we haven't learned the skill of self-observation. And even when we do see our flaws we deny them, sweep them under the carpet or accept them as part of us, 'it's just the way I am'. Only when we can change our behaviour can we stop the rot from setting in.

The enigma that Christ is, exists beyond the physical, emotional and mental bodies of the human condition. To reach that place we must first make a stand against our humanity - by desiring to be greater and commanding that into being.

Just imagine if the whole world took just one day off and sat still in silence with eyes closed, and then contemplated upon the unconditional love of God. I tell you, within twelve months, we would have peace on earth and goodwill to all mankind. Sadly though, people are more interested in their bellies and their careers to be bothered. As you are obviously one of the radical few of God, I ask you to contemplate upon the following two paragraphs:

The word Christ comes from the Greek word Christos, which means 'to know' or 'one who knows'. One who knows, without doubt, that he or she is God.

The love of Jesus the Christ was simply outrageous. I mean, he loved everyone! Could you go up to a thousand strangers, look them in the eyes, and say, "I love you?" Yeshua can. Imagine having such love for self. A man that lived for truth, his truth, in spite of the world. He never lived to be accepted by society. He never needed to be recognised or wanted to be worshipped. He was never that insecure. He never compromised to conform. He knew that when he judged he was being the Son of Man but when he loved unconditionally, he was one with his Father in Heaven, the Son of God. As a man he could do nothing of any significance, on his own. He always acknowledged that it was his Father within him who performed the miracles. And he always displayed his true motives and taught that the Father within him was the same Father God that exists within all of us.

The Blue Window

THE BLUE WINDOW

There are seven windows through which you can view life. To give you some idea of how big God is, take the Milky Way as an example. Our planet is but a speck of dust on the edge of the Milky Way. Now dimensionalise the Milky Way by multiplying it by the power of 50. How big is forever? You should not fear the unknown but be in awe at its sheer size. Now consider how small God is. Take your body and multiply its size by the power of minus 50. If you were the size of your thumb and everything else in your life was scaled down proportionately, how would everything else look? It would, of course, appear the same as it does now. So could a world that is a billion times smaller than this world exist in a faster frequency of infrared light? Of course it can and it does! And what of the other frequencies in the whole of the electromagnetic spectrum of light?

Our journey in consciousness is to open up all seven windows equating our unlimited potentials and unlimited mind. *Unlimited mind and absolute self-love are the same thing.* When we love ourselves absolutely, we realise our greatest potentials and we find that we automatically love everyone else as we love ourselves. Then we are expressing the love of God in human form. Love and acceptance of all, is what being a master is all about.

Looking out of the brown window we see this physical world of body parts, lustful sex and the drive of the animal in us to survive and compete with each other. The red window shows us the world of emotional attachment, with all the self-created demons and phantoms of our mind, trapped discarnate souls and the realm of the antichrist. The yellow window shows us the first window of what we would call paradise or heaven. Souls that are here are more aware, can create their own paradise in the twinkling of an eye, and are destined to return to the brown window because of their 'unfinished business'. These first three windows represent the wheel of reincarnation that we have all been living on for millions of years.

How do we get to the magnificent Blue Window in our current form? Through consciousness of course! How else are we going to do it? Consciousness is everything. Sexuality and controlling others is replaced with love and understanding, so that we feel love for both sexes without any sexual intent. A person of this exquisite consciousness can dance with and embrace another person without sexual intent because they are drunk on love and not drunk on lust or power.

A being of ultra-violet consciousness or above, can participate with others looking through brown, red and yellow tainted glass; without being polluted by the lower consciousness. What distinguishes the being of higher consciousness from the crowd, is simply their loving intent, without any conditions whatsoever; and of course they have no ulterior motives. Physically, they will be in perfect health.

The Blue Window

There is always sacrifice when you decide to accept the ultimate journey of moving to the centre of the labyrinth of your own mind. By the same token, 'becoming blue' requires you to own the first three windows as wisdom; and then choose to close them, never wanting to linger too long in any one of them again. 'Becoming Blue' is moving beyond the 'light body' and its polarised thinking.

We are all here to experience life, certainly. Our souls capture wisdom from the emotional embrace of engaging life's experiences, and there are times when we will want to bathe in the emotion of a dream realised. And so we should. That is being righteous. However, if we want to grow and evolve we must eventually go on to create a new dream. Our enlightenment comes when we close the windows on the past and start a new life that is based in knowledge, and only we will know when we're ready to do that.

You will not permanently close a window until every scrap of wisdom has been gleaned from looking through it. When you realise there is nothing new to learn then you are happy to close the window and move on. In this context, a closed window simply means that you are no longer consciously biased towards living from that lower place. It doesn't mean that you can no longer procreate or feel pain when you stub your toe!

As for me, the content of this book proves that I have been busy observing and experiencing life through the brown, red and yellow windows of the first three seals. Soon I will be ready to consciously experience those deeper aspects of myself that one only gets to experience when the first three windows are closed. One cannot become a wizard if one's energy is still seated 'down below' attracting the lower thoughts forms.

How do we know for certain that other dimensions and worlds exist in a purer consciousness? The only way we can know for certain is to become that purer consciousness. Doubt is a part of the impure consciousness that comprises this world. Our sight, hearing and mobility are limited to this world by virtue of our own polluted consciousness, whereas the purity of a master allows such a being to be truly dimensional, to experience any and all rooms in God's mansion. One can only experience what one is equal to, in terms of the mind of God.

I would like to finish this section of my book on a global note. I have been inspired to do this after listening to Bill Clinton's excellent speech on the David Dimbleby show. In about an hour, Bill summed up how he saw the global arena, our problems past and present; and the solutions and opportunities that beseech each and every one of us. He is living evidence of a man who has obviously learned from his experiences and has thus acquired a degree of wisdom upon reflection of his 12 years in the highest public office.

The Blue Window

I would, however, like to share with you some of the facts that Bill imparted and give a slightly different viewpoint coming from the Blue Window.

Firstly, Bill mentioned that we have a chronic shortage of clean drinking water on the planet and that 25% of our world's population are more susceptible to diseases because of this fact. God's liquid is the most reusable commodity there is and I agree with Bill that the provision of safe drinking water to the whole world should be the utmost priority of any 'global conscious' government. It seems to me that the provision of clean drinking water should naturally go hand in hand with a 'clean up' programme for planet earth.

Bill mentioned that the provision of alternative fuel and energy sources was a multi-billion dollar economy waiting to happen and that some people were in denial of this fact. Correctly or incorrectly, I can only assume that the people in denial are those that have an interest in oil. Further, the love and respect of nature should not be motivated by money but by the love of God.

The leaders of this world are still primarily motivated by money and power, and thus they are not looking through the blue window. A global consciousness that does not look through the blue window will only ever yield a subtle form of tyranny at best. Partnerships with other countries are all very well and good providing the motivation is love and not control. Otherwise, you get an imperialistic dictatorship. It's no good being an advocate of freedom, when at the same time, you know that money from banks, drug companies, construction companies and oil companies; is swaying the voting public. That is manipulation and it makes a political leadership hypocritical.

Bill also talked about the aids crises and how it could go either way. He said it could improve or it could become an epidemic worse than the Black Plaque. I found it interesting that the two worst hit areas of the world are the Caribbean, on America's doorstep, and Russia, on Europe's doorstep. Apparently, according to Bill, a worsening aids crisis would provide fertile ground for terrorism. An interesting association!

Surely what man has created, man can also destroy? That seems to make sense to me. Does that make sense to you? So whilst we are hotly in pursuit of Osama Bin Laden, should we not also be hotly pursuing the perpetrators of other hideous, deadly crimes against humanity? If aids has been man-made then our investigations would need to start with those who are profiting from the human suffering - the shareholders of the drugs companies.

Finally, Bill talked about how we are all children of God on a journey of self-exploration, and that there is no absolute truth. He also talked about how we all

The Blue Window

live in our own self-created, little boxes; even down to what colour tie we prefer to wear! He talked about how the terrorist's hate our truth, whereas we are moving to a position in consciousness (The Blue Window) where our differences are less important than the overall good of the human condition. I would like to endorse wholeheartedly the truth of my brother and add that - as children of God, this also means that we are God, on a spiritual journey to realise this truth in human form.

Our self-created boxes are our sub-personalities that serve only to separate us from our greatness. They are also breeding boxes for all of our diseases. For instance, if Doreen has got cancer but her twin sister Jean is in perfect health, then to get rid of the cancer, Doreen must stop being Doreen and become more like Jean. Those aspects of our personalities that show us looking through the first three windows are the aspects that support all disease, including cancer.

Every box that you have put yourself in, is a construct of your own mind, and is supported neurologically in your brain. If you try to move outside of your boxes, they will remind you of your past and try to contain you there. That emotional bondage can only be satisfied through your redeeming action and that is what continues the vicious, deadly circle. Breaking out of your boxes can only be done by becoming aware of them, observing them at work in your life, understanding them intimately; and finally choosing to starve them through your lack of action and lack of focus upon them.

We have become nothing more than bodies that carry boxes of attitudes. These attitudes represent the very limited intelligence of our animal natures. They cause us to be quick to anger, to judge and blame, to fight and flight, to fear and to be territorial: to be survivalist, sexual creatures that seek money, power and control. When we retire our boxes we gain wisdom and discover we are indeed gods playing out a drama, to further expand ourselves and thus add to the mind of God.

If we are serious about creating a better global consciousness, then its longevity will be determined by our ability to set aside our differences, understand the subjective experience of truth and allow one another those experiences. It's no good that we keep following like lost sheep!

Our salvation lies in our own hands. The lofty truth of another entity is nothing more than philosophy to us, unless we experience the philosophy for ourselves. Then and only then does it become our truth. And it is only our truth that matters to us. Christ may well be sitting at the centre of the labyrinth of our own minds, but we can only go there with knowledge. It is knowledge that delivers us and brings us to that sweet point of surrender. It matters not that our truth may differ from others. Brick by brick we must build our temples in consciousness. We may not be master craftsmen but we can all build our temples with the bricks of our

The Blue Window

own truth. Patience is the mortar. Replacing the past with love is a long, arduous process and a diligent consistent effort is required.

I endorse what Bill Clinton has said when I say that working together in constructive, global partnerships, is more important than the petty differences that have separated us; because of our own lack of wisdom. Let us all accept that each and every one of us is different, and was created that way for the acquisition of our own truth. Never again can we let somebody else's ignorant opinions undermine our truth but rather we must stand up and live our truth; and respect everybody else's free will to do the same. At the end of the day, we either stay being body-conscious mortals or we become super-conscious immortals. We cannot be both at the same time! Super-consciousness is the state we attain upon the permanent retirement of our body-conscious, boxes of limitation.

This society is the one big box that contains all the little boxes that you and I readily create and identify as being what we are. For one to live in such a society and yet break out of the big box, takes incredible courage because it takes a dogged determination to internally change oneself, against the reflection of a mirrored consciousness constantly pressing to limit one's mind. Sooner or later, one of us will make the home run and a real master will once again be realised in human flesh.

We do not want the evolving of just one person to such greatness, only to then hate him or her because they represent everything we have not aspired to. No, if such a person ever emerges again from the soup of humanity, then we should be inspired by our own acceptance of our own equality with him or her. We can never fail our own acceptance; providing we understand that our doubt is just another one of our limiting boxes.

The ambition of any world leadership wishing to have a sustainable, successful, global consciousness should be to gradually move that collective consciousness to the blue window. A carefully engineered education process, starting in the western world, can bring this about. When the poorer nations get to experience the loving generosity of the wealthy nations, without any conditions whatsoever, then global attitudes will start to change and become more giving and more allowing. Being demanding, creating conditions and creating indebtedness, is not the way forward. History has already proven that. The only way we are going to permanently rid ourselves of the threat of terrorism and the threat of a massive natural disaster, is to individually and thus collectively move our consciousness to the Blue Window. So be it!

Part 3

Becoming a Master

INTRODUCTION

It's the 20th October 2002 and it's taken me over a year to get around to writing the third part of this book. To be honest with you, I've had a shit year! All self-created of course! I've struggled to maintain gainful employment, I've messed my partner about and I've had some pretty ugly stuff to look at about myself and my behaviour. But then I know this is all the friction and fire necessary to purge myself from my past, so that I can have a cleaner, more joyful future.

Before I continue with my epilogue, what has prompted me to continue with this book, is the despair of a close friend who has recently lost her mother and is struggling to come to terms with the effect this has had on her life. So I am taking this opportunity to continue my work with my friend in mind, addressing some of her issues whilst holding true my message to a wider audience. My close friend is around 53 years of age, an only child and married with two grown-up daughters; who are also married with children.

I think it is fair for me to say that most parents who have just one child, pour a considerable amount of love into the child and this can be equally from both parents or more dominant from one of them. In general, I think it is also fair for me to say that you women tend to be able to feel love and express love more freely than us men do. It's not that we don't love, but that we have not allowed ourselves (because of a lack of self-love) to express our love for you. This, then, is an evolutionary opportunity for us all to feel love for ourselves and for other people, and to freely express it.

To my friend. You haven't spoken to me much about your father but I do know you were very close to your mother, and in your own words, you have said that she was the one person who you felt really loved you and that you could talk to. I don't doubt this to be the case and that you really miss that close bonding and communication with her. Your need to be loved by someone is now greater than ever. Of course, the need was always there but it was not as obvious as it is now, because your mother always fulfilled it.

Now she has once again shed the physical body and made the transition to consciously occupying one of her 'other' bodies, the one best suited to her level of consciousness. So it is that her level of mind determines which body she is now consciously occupying, and this is consistent with the atmosphere she is now

Becoming a Master

enjoying. She will be where she is equal to consciously. This is why the knowledge contained in this book is so valuable - from my experience I know that it consciously advances every individual who reads it.

In the absence of your mother, it must be like a vacuum has left a gaping hole in your life. As painful as it must be, it has identified a need in you that you can choose to continue to suffer from or eventually choose to heal.

As you know, some people choose to continue their suffering and it becomes part of their identity. They even hold onto things that remind them of the past, so as to continue to suffer way beyond even what our conditioned society considers to be normal. If they are not careful, pain and suffering become so imbedded in them that it is difficult to let go of these emotional feelings. The feelings become a part of them, and then it takes a considerable effort to change and heal. It is said that time is a great healer but it is not so much the passing of time but the changing of one's mind that causes healing to occur.

Before I continue I want to clarify the literal meaning of what becoming a Christ means, as I learned it from Ramtha. Jesus became a Christ because he allowed his body to die (it was his choice to be crucified) and then he resurrected his body from death and he ascended. It was his final initiate test, which he successfully completed by defying death through the willpower of his mind. Ramtha and other masters have proven that it is not necessary for one's body to firstly die before one can ascend. And as ascension is the goal here, this Part 3 is now called Becoming a Master (the first attempt at this book was entitled Becoming a Christ).

BECOMING A MASTER

I spent a few days on my own in Scotland, and whilst I was driving the 500 mile trek back home, I was thinking about myself, my relationship with others and my relationship to God. I passed a coach moving in the opposite direction and a pebble or stone hit my windscreen. Fortunately, my windscreen remained intact and strong. 'Just like God', I thought. Had my windscreen shattered into thousands of little pieces, all scattered across the highway; would each piece of glass know it is a piece of glass and a part of a stronger, more powerful structure? Your answer would probably be, 'of course glass doesn't know it's glass', but is that the correct answer?

Just because something doesn't think, it does not mean it's not self-aware. Does a tree know it's a tree? A valid question don't you think? Everything that exists is made up of energy and energy is consciousness in motion, even when it has coagulated to form a solid-appearing mass.

So a shattered piece of glass probably does know it is glass and certainly a tree would know it is a tree. And can God be found in the glass and in the tree? Absolutely! God **is** the glass and the tree and everything else that exists because God **is** the foundation of everything and everything is an expressive form of God. So why do we not know we are God? Are we lesser than a piece of glass or a tree? Or is it because of what we have been taught by the ignorant, religious men?

What about love? What about it? Does God love you? *The mere fact that you suck air is evidence of God's love for you.* You wouldn't exist if God didn't love you because God is love and what is love can only love. If God did not love all of its creations, it would not love itself and therefore it would not exist in any form, because all form is loving-energy, coagulated. Simply, none of us would exist without the love of God. It is love that allows us to live upon a platform of life that is also held together by love. God is love and God is everything that exists, past, present and future. Nothing exists outside of the providence of God.

So God loves you and I, and now that I know I am God, I love you too, but only of course to the extent that I love myself. Love is only ever fractured when we think we are separate from God, and thus separate from other people. So when we ask the question 'does God love me?', we should really be asking, 'do I love myself?', because it really is the same question.

It is not the responsibility of someone else to love us, but it is our responsibility to love ourselves. And we can only love others to the extent we love ourselves. To say that we love our children greater than we love ourselves, is not the truth, because in a greater sense, they are us and we are them. What we love about our

Becoming a Master

little children is they represent our hope for a brighter future and they are living a dream that somehow we got lost in. They are doing what we never had the chance to do or were never brave enough to do. It is we who have stopped living and so live our lives through them. And they grow up, fly from the nest and we try to hold on to them, because it is just another part of our self-created identity.

Where do we go from here? There is only ever two options (no matter how much counselling one has!), an evolutionary one and a non-evolutionary one. We either give up our suffering and start living again or we die clutching onto the past. Those who we mourn have now left us, but they will come again and play at another time, as sure as night follows day.

Our biggest challenge in life is to get rid of our self-created identities. When we have always been somebody's daughter, somebody's mother and somebody's wife; then events that shatter those images will leave us utterly lost and in despair. But when we have knowledge and we consciously take these badges off, then we are once again venturing into the unknown and evolving spiritually. It is a brave person who retires past self-serving identities in favour of the unknown, but the reward is an evolutionary leap that will save lifetimes of repetitive experiences.

Back to the plot! There are three stages that we go through at every step of our evolutionary growth. They are:

1. The gaining of knowledge, which is either an undisputable fact or a lofty philosophy yet to be experienced.

2. The acceptance and integration of that knowledge through life's experiences, which then becomes the individual's personal truth.

3. The letting go of the old belief systems, which were acquired when one was most vulnerable, in favour of the 'higher' truth that one has 'realised'.

If we have the knowledge but we do not accept it or we deny it, because we are not open-minded or brave enough to experience it; then it will only ever remain an intellectual philosophy of somebody else's truth and not ours. If, however, we know it as our truth yet we still hold onto the past, because of our fears or our addictions, then we are a house divided against itself and run the risk of being a hypocrite at times. Living our truth therefore becomes paramount in importance.

Understanding and accepting we are God, and that our evolutionary journey is nothing more than a journey of self-exploration and self-love, is fundamental to our evolutionary progress. We are not here to be a 'somebody', but are here to understand that really we are a 'nobody' (please refer to my article 'To be a

Becoming a Master

Somebody or a Nobody?' from my book entitled 'Inspirational Articles of Wisdom'), and all we have to do is pursue the path that brings us joy; regardless of what other people are thinking and doing. This, of course, is much easier said than done!

Where is God in all of this? Right inside each and every one of us, observing our emotional dramas, wondering when we are going to turn the page and start a new page in our book of life. Most of us have been stuck on the same page for lifetimes! Is it any wonder we are bored and boring?

My recent trip to Scotland revealed to me many aspects of my personality that I found hard to accept, hard to admit to, hard to chew on and particularly hard to reveal to others. Also, I had come to realise that each and everyone of us has an ulterior motive, unconsciously at work in our lives. And it is so powerful that it can remain successfully undercover, at work in our lives, completely undetected. Without spiritual training, such as I received at Ramtha's school, what chance do we all have?

In my case, it was enough for me to realise that all of my adult life, I had been nothing more than a sexual predator, preying upon as many beautiful women as I could to satisfy my seemingly insatiable sexual appetite. To understand that everything in my life had been primarily motivated by this strong undercurrent, which I wasn't fully aware of, and how it was also the reason for my lack of accomplishment; was really quite devastating for me. Well, mine is out of the closet now and so the question is - what are your ulterior motives? You need to identify them and reveal them, if you want to heal and progress spiritually...

I came back from Scotland feeling a complete and utter failure, and realised that in the eyes of the world, I am a failure. But then I reasoned it was o.k. to be a failure because if there were no failures, there would be no successes either, as they are opposite poles of the same ideal, driven by society. I told myself that for every success there are many more failures but I still felt like crap!

When I finally picked myself up from the gutter and dusted off my jeans, I realised that now I had *learned* from the experience; it can no longer be regarded as a failure. And even though it took 25 years of screwing around, what's that in the light of all eternity? Anyway, how can a god be a failure? It is simply not possible when that god knows that this life is an illusion, created to evoke emotion for the purpose of capturing the emotion as wisdom for the soul.

Just like the pieces of shattered glass, we are all unique, individualised, expressions of God. Indeed, Ramtha calls us the 'forgotten gods' who made the journey here, and after a time, got lost in our illusions and eventually forgot about

Becoming a Master

our true divinity. What makes us individuals is our free will to choose our destiny and a soul that records our unique journeys and presses us to complete our books of evolution. **Everyone's journey is unique and equally important.**

Collectively, we are all a part of the great spirit, which lives both inside of us and is all around us. It is that part of us which observes everything we say and do, yet it is totally detached from all of the emotional dramas, which comprise the human experience.

The physical body is simply the vehicle that we wear and via its senses, it allows us to interact emotionally with our environment. The body is a genetic match for the incoming soul and its unfinished business here. However, as time goes by, it develops its own mindset and agenda, relating to the first three seals of polarised 'human' consciousness; and this is passed on genetically at conception to the next generation. Daunting isn't it?!

What is it then to become a master and how do we go about becoming it? It is all about choice. Choosing to live in accordance with a new understanding instead of living in accordance with the past, is the key. All I can endeavour to do is to try and help to create that understanding in you, and accept that it will always be your free will to choose what reality you get to experience. Becoming a master is about achieving and maintaining a level of consciousness that is unpolluted by human consciousness. For instance, there is no room for tyranny or victimisation in unconditional love. Neither is there any room for pain and suffering or lustful sex for that matter. That doesn't mean to say that Masters cannot make love to their partners or suffer from pain; Yeshua and Mary were great examples of that!

To achieve a consciousness of unconditional love one has to return to a wholesome consciousness. At the Blue level there is no gender bias! The deity Shiva represents a blue-bodied entity. Shiva is neither male nor female but both! The ignorant amongst you will interpret this as homosexuality and lesbianism but in fact it is neither. A non-sexual bias is taken by a wise being who has explored themselves sexually and has chosen to give up what it is to be a man or woman in favour of realising greater truths and thus experiencing greater realities.

It is an ignorant person who chooses to live a celibate lifestyle from the outset because truth is only realised through experience. And so the spiritual journey can only be completed by one who 'lives' life; not by one who abstains from it.

It is not about denial coupled with regret. It is a conscious, wilfull act, when one is ready to let go off the past. How long does it take for one to arrive at such a place in one's own mind? How long is a piece of string? I guess it is when one has had enough of living in the carnal mind.

Becoming a Master

First of all you have to gain the knowledge. Secondly, your open-minded acceptance of the possibilities that the knowledge engenders in you, sets the wheels in motion for you to experience it. As Ramtha says, once you say 'I accept' then you are on automatic pilot! Your truth comes through experiencing the knowledge in your life. Finally, there is the letting go of the past in favour of the unknown. This is difficult because there are no precedents in the conscious brain for what is subconscious in you. It is all within you, but it is for you to make it conscious, indeed, for you to make it known.

Let us take a look at this a little more closely. To gain in knowledge and truth requires one to have an open mind, a rarity in human consciousness. If people will not open themselves up 'to know' then they, by their own choice, are their own worst enemy. Thankfully, for humanity, we have a few people, like yourself, who are open-minded enough to at least read this book and probably other books of a similar ilk. The pursuit of knowledge and the gaining of understanding can take many years but what else is there that is more important? I hope this book will spur you on to investigate further some of the material I have touched upon.

The reason it is so difficult to 'live' your evolving personal truth at times, is because your new understandings will uproot every previously held idea you had about yourself; your self-created image of God (which is far removed from the whole truth) and the nature of reality: which you thought was fixed and its not! The new understandings will literally turn your world upside down and throw your life into chaos. Your past demons will fight to hold onto you and at times you will feel like ending it all! Know that out of chaos eventually comes clarity.

Why would we want to hold onto the past? Because it is known, it is familiar, it is comfortable, it is our self-created identity and we are addicted emotionally to it. You don't believe me? Try and give it up then you'll know what I mean. You may have several attempts before you realise the more you try to let go of your past the more your demons are upon you.

We finally realise we are addicted to human behaviour and we fear our own greatness. Are we prepared to give up everything that constitutes being human and stand alone, as an example of what is possible when we accept our own divinity?

To start with, very few people will become such immaculate individuals. However, eventually, Christ-like beings will be an accepted reality here; then everybody will realise it is a potential that exists within them, and a probability that, by individual's choosing, can become a certainty.

The hardest challenge in life is not being a success in the eyes of society but is facing yourself in your quest for self-mastery. Therein lies your greatness.

Becoming a Master

THE SECRET OF HAPPINESS

At the time of writing, I had just returned from a skiing holiday in the Alps, along with a few friends. At the dinner table, on the second evening, one of my friends said to me 'I just want to be happy'. This got me thinking about how we would need to change to become happy and how we can all be happy. Certainly, the desire to be happy is what sets the wheels of this reality into motion.

Many years ago I did a 'Mind Powers' course, which was a self-development type course lasting a few days. During the course, the course leader said to all of us, 'who wants to know the secret of happiness?' You can imagine the whole audience put their hands up including myself! The course leader then said, 'the secret of happiness is to **be** happy; it is no more than having a happy attitude'.

Well, I know that 'attitude is everything' but is it really as simple as having a happy attitude? Certainly, a happy disposition helps with one's approach towards life and I know of many 'happy go lucky' people who appear to be happy and friendly all of the time. However, is their appearance really evidence of a joyful being or is it an image they are portraying to others? In other words, is it a surface condition or is it real joy emanating from their being?

It has been said that to have a successful life you have to 'do whatever it is you want to do that makes you happy'. Is happiness then just doing whatever it is that makes you happy? Because if it is, you would constantly need to be 'doing' to make yourself happy and perhaps never realise a state of happiness that is unaffected by what's happening in your life. It would be like being on a treadmill constantly pursuing events that create happiness in your life. Perhaps this is happiness but then it would be a temporary emotional state and certainly different to the state of joy experienced by enlightened beings.

To my mind, what we really want to achieve in our lives is to live in a state of bliss and to be filled with joy. This is a state of being that we can only achieve when we eliminate every source of unhappiness from our lives. And the sources of our unhappiness include our compromises, our untruths, our fears, our judgements, our ulterior motives and our inability to find forgiveness for ourselves and for others. Indeed, any act or omission that is not motivated by love.

Eliminating the sources of our unhappiness requires us to move beyond the human, emotional condition. All our fears are emotional; they are nothing more than demons in our minds. For example, the fear of being 'out of control' on the ski slopes prevents one from engaging in a joyous activity. Equally, the need to feel 'safe' holds one back in life generally, and any resulting compromises can be seen in the body.

Becoming a Master

CULTIVATE YOUR MIND

So it is your mind that is creating your reality. If your reality is humdrum then what does that tell you about the state of your mind? If you want a greater reality then you obviously have to develop a greater mind. It is your brain that facilitates your mind and every able body has the same brain capacity. Your brain can facilitate all of the seven levels of consciousness (the seven seals described earlier) to the degree you are willing to open yourself up to those loftier thoughts.

Cultivating your mind is like trying to grow the most beautiful flowerbed on a piece of land that has been used as a rubbish tip. First of all, you have to get rid of the rubbish from the past. Then you dig and weed the soil to prepare it to receive your seeds. Before you plant your seeds you have obviously envisioned what your flowerbed will look like. You plant your seeds and nurture them until they flower. It is the same with your mind. If you are holding onto the emotional garbage from your past then you'll never clear your mind, to be able to plant the flowers for your future. You won't even find the time to think about cultivating your dreams, if your mind is full of recycled trash from your past.

God is pressing to you all seven levels of consciousness, for you to receive, to experience and to intimately understand. With your brain you have the faculty to gather mind. Let me remind you of what tools you have got to tend your garden:

1.   Invest in yourself

In the last two decades I have spent thousands of pounds investing in self-development courses, tapes, videos and books of an esoteric nature. For a period of eleven years I attended an Ancient School of Wisdom (Ramtha's school of Enlightenment), twice yearly at overseas venues. I have made a considerable investment in cultivating my mind. What percentage of your income have you invested in developing yourself? Please go and work it out.

2.   Do as the Master does

Apparently, Jesus the Christ, said to his God everyday 'beloved God, open me up to know'. How else are you going to develop a relationship with God, if you don't talk to that higher principle in you? You can't build trust without firstly developing a personal relationship.

3.   Become the Observer

We are all wading in the river of emotion, and it is our environment that keeps triggering the feelings we get. We then associate the feelings as being us. For

Becoming a Master

example, 'I am feeling sad or I am feeling insecure' are mind associations. We have to firstly disassociate ourselves from these feelings by becoming the 'observer'. If you are observing yourself being angry then there is a part of you that is observing and not being angry; as distinctly separate from the part of you that is embroiled in the anger. The 'observer' is the god part in you. It is completely detached from any emotional reactions, which are simply chemical reactions happening in your body.

Becoming the observer of your life is a first step. You can then observe all of your rubbish and keep looking at it until you uncover the flaws in your own psyche. When you have found the weeds, it is up to you whether you dig them up or continue to let them spoil your view. For instance, as a child I was always frightened of the dark, and even as an adult I was uncomfortable on my own in a darkened room. Yet after a period of deep contemplation on the matter, I finally found the event that was causing my reaction.

When I was a child of about four years of age, I stayed up late one night and watched a horror film with my father. It was about Medusa, the snake-headed gorgon; and I believed my father when he told me that if one looked upon her face, one would turn into stone! Uncovering the weed made me realise I was never frightened of the dark but rather I was frightened of what I might see and what might happen to me as a result. I then had the choice to unseat the power this belief had over me or leave the weed to impair my vision.

Isn't it the case that we say, 'ignorance is bliss' because we are frightened of what we might see and get to know?

When you become the observer, you eventually get to see all of your past emotional garbage and you keep looking at it until you get every scrap of wisdom you can get from it. You will know when you've turned that old lead of your humanity into your golden, spiritual body of truth.

When you've got your truth, you can then dispose of the feelings by becoming resolute in your truth. Keep reminding the feelings that you have the truth and they are the lies. Command them to die!

These weeds will keep growing back if you let them. You have to keep on top of the situation and let them know that you are the one sitting upon the golden throne of your mind. It is a battle that you can only win by accepting you are the observer and not your body's chemical, emotional voices.

When you, as the observer, are continually observing yourself being the observer; then you have moved to the other side of the emotional river and are looking

Becoming a Master

through the blue window. As you gain in wisdom, you emotionally detach and in the place of those past feelings you find a tranquillity and a love that is beyond words. I am not wishing to imply here that emotions are 'bad'! Indeed, they are the derivatives of the experiences that are necessary to capture wisdom.

4. Do your loving affirmations everyday

Please see my article 'Dispelling the Genetic Myth' for information on how and why affirmations work. Here are a few to get you started:

I am observing my life through the blue window
I am perfectly healthy through each evolving moment
I am the master of my emotions
I am no longer my past, it is no more in me
I am patient and calm at all times
I am responsible for all aspects of my life
I am complete
I am healthy, wealthy and wise

Please remember to effect a change in your reality, your conscious mind must match your subconscious mind; the two minds must become one. It therefore takes a conscious effort as well as subconscious re-programming.

5. Learn how to do C&E breathing

You will dramatically accelerate your growth if you learn to do Consciousness and Energy Breathing and practice it on a regular basis. C&E breathing can literally take you into the higher echelons of thought, thus opening your mind up to what is currently subconscious in you. All of your answers are within you and this technique helps to bring them out! It is an amazing experience and a must for any serious student of the Great Work. The technique is explained in the Ramtha book 'A Beginner's Guide to Creating Reality' available from www.ramtha.com and is taught at the school's beginning retreats.

6. Watch your attitude

You cannot become wise and enlightened by abstaining from life. And you cannot live life without interacting with other people. How you interact with others is evidence of your behaviour and is a reflection of your attitude towards them and yourself. Your daily behaviour then, is determined by your attitude, and this mirrors back to you where you are at, as a conscious being.

If you wake up in the morning with a bad attitude then you start the day off on

Becoming a Master

the wrong footing, and the day is unlikely to improve as it unfolds. Getting out of bed and hating everybody around you is a mirror image of your own lack of self-love. Why do you hate other people and thus yourself? You need to uncover this weed and pull it out of your mind!

When I was a child, if I got out of bed in the morning with a 'cob on' then my mother used to send me back to bed with instructions to get out of bed on the other side! My experience tells me that it's vitally important to start the day off on the correct footing. Try waking up just fifteen minutes earlier, sit up in bed but keep your eyes closed. See yourself having a wonderful day, meeting new people, and being presented with new opportunities for personal growth. It really does work. If you do your affirmations as well, you'll probably be ready to take on the whole world by the time you've had breakfast!

Don't worry about what other people think. What do they really know about you and your truth? They're not inside your head so don't buy into their opinions about you. Just focus upon yourself and understand that you are accumulating your truth as you go along and that's all that matters at the end of the day.

7.   **Never, ever, give up on your dreams**

Your dreams are composed of holographic images. And thoughts are the firing of holographic images upon the frontal lobe of your brain. All conscious thoughts are alive. Your dreams are always alive and well in you, unless you annihilate them with the destructive thoughts of doubt.

Never carve your dreams up by putting conditions on them, such as, a time limit in which they must materialise. Keep them pure and hold onto them with a vice grip. Know, without doubt, that one-day you will be in your dream, when you least expect it to happen. It doesn't matter whether your dreams materialise in this lifetime or in another lifetime. If you keep them firmly on your timeline and you keep walking forward and evolving yourself, you will definitely be in your dream one-day - I promise you.

The answers to your questions and to the bare mysteries of this life are often to be found in your most bizarre dreams. Just because what you dream of, may not be of this world, does not negate the probability of it happening in another time and place; when you're ready to visit. Patience is the key ingredient here.

8.   **When you're ready - retire your emotional needs**

We are nothing more than phantoms playing out a drama. The observer in us, that which is our true self, has created phantoms and sent them forth into this world

Becoming a Master

for the purpose of emotional experience. The phantom therefore is the basis of our experience here. The reason we say this life is an illusion is because the basis of the reality we have created here; is not to be found in our true self but the power is in a phantom that creates reality amongst other phantoms: by way of each placing memory in each other.

So the basis of my reality here is not in myself but in my family and friends who I have placed memories with. And the reason I have done this is to create identities with other people that give me a sense of self, albeit that I now know this to be illusionary. To two people I have been their son and they have been my parents. To others I have been their friends and to a few I have been their enemies. I have been sick and broke and other phantoms have taken pity on me. Now I help people to heal. The list goes on and includes every emotional experience.

The point is this. We create our reality in other people and they in us. We give to them memory to the extent that we know they can handle it. In other words, we only tell them what we know we can tell them without them blowing a fuse. So the whole gambit of our life, indeed our complete image is spread amongst everyone and everything in our lives and we visit them to keep reaffirming our self-created identity of self. This is the reason why we are always keen to replace somebody in our life who is no longer there yet they were fulfilling a need in us.

In truth, we are all looking for 'the one', the so-called soulmate who we can confide in and tell it all to; not realising that they don't exist because everybody else is a phantom too! And everybody else is doing the same thing. We are all phantoms trying to hold together an image that serves us to be that way.

If you and I removed the memory we have with other people, by no longer having any interactions with them, then who would we be? If nobody knew we were this way or that way, then would we be this way or that way? The answer is no because the reality of being a certain way is in them and not in us. It is the memory we have placed in them that we have to keep visiting so as to reaffirm our illusionary sense of self.

The progressive redefining of self is nothing more than the stripping of the phantom and its illusionary images, until it is bare in front of us and we can see right through it. Now the power is no longer with the phantom…

What does this mean in practical terms? It means that we need to examine the reasons why everybody who is in our life, is in our life? It is no good for us to simply say, 'it's because they are my mother or it's because they are my son or my best friend'. All of those relationships are part of the image that you and I, as phantoms, have created. It is all a grand illusion.

Becoming a Master

We therefore need to dig a bit deeper. For instance, if you think you're all grown up but you're still living at home with mum and dad or you can't go a week without seeing or talking with one of your parents (or children for that matter); then ask yourself these questions. Why is this person in my life? What emotional need do they fulfill in me and me in them? What really is the true basis of the relationship I have with them? What are my emotional needs?

The same rationale applies to your friends, your lovers and anyone else who is regularly in your life. What is the real basis of the relationship? Why is this person in your life? Why do you have anything to do with them? What is your emotional need? Is it financial dependence? Is it guilt? Is it because they pity you or you pity them? Is it a sexual need? Is it because they compliment you? Is it because they treat you how you want to be treated? Is it because you can easily exploit them? Is it because you can use and abuse them and they still keep coming back for more? Is it because you are frightened to be on your own?

The answer is to identify your emotional needs and then you retire them. It's not that you have to kick everyone out of your life and live like a hermit, although certainly you will have fewer people in your life as a result of retiring your emotional needs. It is more the case that you will change the basis of your relationships with others from a state of emotional need to one of unconditional love. You may say, 'I love him or I love her', but is it love without any conditions whatsoever or is it really that you need them in your life to confirm your own identity?

Becoming a Master

A NEW LIFE

We are all here, individually and collectively, to evolve ourselves and thus humanity as a whole, beyond our existing known boundaries. This means that individually we are to change from our existing state of being to become a higher, more evolved state of being.

As discussed earlier, our existing personalities are a combination of our inherited genes and the social conditioning of the society in which we live. Different cultures impose different conditioning upon the minds of their citizens by virtue of their way of life. It all amounts to a limitation of mind.

To change from the personality we've 'picked up' into a new personality of our own design, is the evolutionary task we all face. This is a task that flies in the face of family, tradition, culture, religion, colour, status, wealth, fashion, gender, fame etc.; indeed: it flies in the face of all the accepted values in our societies.

Never before have we been given so much knowledge to challenge our inherited belief systems and to intimidate the self-imposed limitations of our minds. How we develop into the future can only be limited by our own level of acceptance and our own willingness to let go of the past. And our unwillingness to let go of the past is evidence of our own lack of understanding or outright stubbornness towards change.

What we need to develop is our own ideal, not one that we have been conditioned to accept but one that is our own creation. How do we want to be? Notice I didn't say what role or status do we want to play or achieve within an existing framework. We are not here to simply fit in with modern-day society, although our politicians would want us to think that way!

Evolution is not about being accepted by an existing image but is about changing and moving beyond the boundaries of that accepted image; the exact image that is pressed to us everyday by mind-control techniques, which company advertising and marketing is so good at.

So we must become like the caterpillar that transforms itself into the beautiful butterfly. The caterpillar represents the old personality and the butterfly represents a new life that has yet to unfold. In evolutionary terms, we are all the same as the caterpillar that has yet to embark upon its remarkable transformation.

We can never evolve beyond our own level of acceptance. Very few people will be able to accept that they can be a master until they witness, first hand, somebody else being in that state of purity. Even then their own acceptance will rely on their

Becoming a Master

acceptance of equality with the Christ-like personality. One's understanding and acceptance of the story of involution (described in detail in 'A Beginner's Guide to Creating Reality') is essential to this acceptance of equality.

Your ideal is not supposed to fit any existing image because that is just image worship. What is important is that your ideal is greater than your past and that you genuinely strive to become it. It is far greater to have an ideal that you struggle to become than have no ideal at all or one that represents no more than social acceptance.

Once the template has been designed in your mind then the individual components can be formulated and worked upon. These are the elements of the Great Work that spiritual masters have spoken about.

A diligent effort is required to replace the demons from your past thinking. Only when the new knowledge is added to the quagmire of your mind, will the alchemical process start to take place. The metamorphosis of the caterpillar is likened to the human alchemical process of turning the lead of the past into the gold of spiritual truth.

Whether it is the raising of the Phoenix from the ashes, the emergence of the butterfly from the caterpillar or the flight of a dove, it's all symbolic of one thing - the flight of FREEDOM.

Becoming a master is the ultimate ideal from the point of view of humanity. It is the crowning glory. Any climb down from that point is a compromise to any evolved mind. At the same time, we must realise that our own evolution progresses at the rate of our own acceptance of new knowledge and its integration into our lives, which can only come from our own desires and willingness to open ourselves up 'to know'.

A friend once said to me, 'you can do anything'. This I found to be inspiring but is it a question of what we can do or what we can be? For instance, can we train our minds to be everything and nothing at the same time, just like God is? Or is our viewpoint always going to be limited by our own design? We are the creators of our future destiny - be in no doubt about that!

Designing a new life for yourself that bears no resemblance to your past and then choosing to live as the butterfly instead of continuing to be a caterpillar, is a hard task indeed. Why is this? It is because change is uncomfortable, not only for yourself but also for those who observe it in you. You are moving forward in your life and they are standing still. They can no longer relate to you because you are at a loftier vantage point and you have to continue to play the game with them, if you

Becoming a Master

still want them in your life. Can you really afford to compromise or do you fly away and leave them standing in their own confusion, hoping that one day they will follow your lead?

The more spiritually advanced we become the more difficult we find it is to fit in with the accepted values of society. We eventually reach a point when we cease trying to 'fit in' and realise it is only our truth that matters to us.

In the absence of your own ideal, there is one ideal that you can focus upon, which is not currently in abundance in human consciousness. It is unconditional Love. Moving your mind to the blue window can be the structure (the skeleton if you like) of the butterfly you are trying to unfold from within. In love there is no lack; there is not the loss of energy that occurs when the energy is split into polarities.

In practice, being more loving is a matter of changing one's attitude. For instance, can you replace a lustful attitude with a loving one? You can if it is your will to do so. Can you move beyond your pain and suffering? You can if it is your will to do so. Can you let go of your need to be controlled or to be in control? You can always let go if you love unconditionally. Whatever you are perplexed by in your life, you will always find the answer in love. Are you looking out of the blue window or is your view blinded by the light (the yellow window)?

Life then is not about you acquiring more and more money or your sex life or being a somebody or keeping up with the Jones's or living to be acceptable to others and to your society. No, it is really about fulfilling the journey of your soul in its quest for self-mastery.

Becoming a Master

AND FINALLY

Why would I, you or indeed anybody else want to do this spiritual journey and become a master? Because becoming a master is the only path to freedom! Every other path leads to certain death, and in most cases, yet another blind re-entry into this shadowy world with its anti-Christ consciousness.

So, in a nutshell, what really is this ultimate journey? It is a journey of self-love from conditioned mind to unlimited mind. We can easily judge ourselves all day long but can we set aside our judgements and love ourselves all day long? Because that is what it takes.

Becoming a master and becoming unlimited in your mind are the same thing.

You can look at other people and see they grow old and die, but what do they know? If you think it is inevitable that you are going to grow old and die, is that not a limitation in your mind? And would that not therefore be your reality? Of course it is and it would. This is not a complicated science!

The only difference between you and a master is the master understands life, and in particular, they understand the science of life; namely, Quantum Mechanics. They understand that everyday they wake up in a quantum world full of unlimited potentials. And they also understand that the potentials that will manifest in their life will depend entirely upon how they are observing life. In other words, their reality reflects where their focus is. It is exactly the same for all of us.

The master knows that reality and truth are subjective experiences and that one person may have an ugly reality and another may have a beautiful reality, dependent only upon how they are viewing life. The master knows that reality can only conform to a person's common thought and thus they have refined their thought processes to reflect the reality they want to intentionally create.

It is true that the temptations of this world are everywhere and ever-present, but does that mean we have to go down those roads? Everyday we are faced with choices and our lives become the choices we make. A great being is one who consciously makes choices in the direction they want to go in, and is no longer tempted by the demons of their past.

It follows then, that if we want to progress ourselves and consciously evolve, then we have to make very different choices from those we have made in the past. In other words, we have to change our behaviour from our past behaviour. This, of course, starts with a change of mind and is fundamentally a decision to be greater than our self-created, self-imposed limitations.

Becoming a Master

Let me give you a quick example: - If we believe somebody has wronged us then we have two options in our mind. We can either judge the other person or forgive them. Humanity likes to sit in judgement; it is our sense of illusionary power and what also enslaves us. By sitting in judgement we have given our power away. If, on the other hand, we find forgiveness in our hearts, which obviously comes from love, then we are free of the situation. Simple isn't it? In reality we only ever find forgiveness when we understand…

Can you please now grab a piece of paper and a writing instrument?

Draw a small circle in the centre of the paper and put inside it the word God. Now draw a larger broken circle around it, putting the word Phantom in the space between the two rings. This represents the sum total of the make-up of you. The outer ring is broken because it is only temporal. It is that aspect of you, the Phantom in you, which takes you to the grave every lifetime. However, if the Phantom is stripped bare, then the god that you are, recalls the Phantom and all that is left is the permanence of the inner ring - God expressing through human form, indeed, you as a master!

Please be aware that when you go through the process of unfolding back through the seals, the energy that you have expended on the 'lower' seals will eventually all come back to you. However, this power can only come back in the form that it was given out. In other words, tyrannical behaviour towards another can only return as tyrannical energy and you will feel the impact of that. For more on this listen to the Ramtha CDs 'The Planes of Bliss'.

It is important that when you are ready to undergo this process, that you become the observer, and are thus calm enough to 'hold your nerve'. The only way you can successfully cross the troubled waters is to keep your focus on the distant shore. For a new energy to form the old energy has to die, and as it dies, there will be chaos in your life. But when the chaos subsides and you come out of the fire, you will be one with your God. The caterpillar has shed its past and the beautiful butterfly is born...

And finally, if you want to embark upon this journey, be aware that it can be a perilous journey at times. This is not because anything awful is going to happen to you, but is because there are many pitfalls that you can easily fall into, metaphorically speaking. At times you will feel lost and bewildered, because you will not know where you are at, in relation to your progress through the seven seals. It is like walking through a labyrinth, blindfolded!

When God surfaces in your life, so will the Phantom be evident in your mind. At times you will find it difficult to discern the two, because the Phantom can be

Becoming a Master

very subtle and very clever at times. It will always move to hold its illusionary self together. So to start with you will follow the Phantom back to your past, but in time, you will become wise to this creature and with self-discipline you will reign it in; and thus you will stand steadfast with your God. You have to emotionally starve this creature until it dies. It's the only way forward because the phantom in you feeds on emotion.

Here is a simple example. Let us take the emotion known as disappointment. All of us have felt disappointed at times but why is that? Does God ever feel disappointed with any of its creation? No! It simply loves all of its creation. So why do we feel disappointed? Because at times we do not love. We place expectations on ourselves and on others, and obviously most of the time these expectations are not met. And so the placing of expectations on ourselves or onto others is the phantom at work, because how can they or we possibly meet all of our expectations all of the time? The phantom then is that which is not loving; it is the anti-Christ: whereas Christ consciousness exemplifies the love of God.

When you are feeling disappointed you are in the yellow window (the third seal), whereas knowledge gives you the choice of being either yellow or blue (the fourth seal). That is how close God is in your life. It is simply a matter of changing your mind... and then the change of attitude follows...

You cannot know what it is like to be a master in advance because it is not an intellectual understanding. And neither is it an image that some people foolishly portray that they are. The only way you can know what it is like to be a master, is to be it and that is the start of a long, arduous journey of self-discovery.

God says to you, 'go forth and create from me whatever you want. Create from the thought that I am, then experience the reality of your creations and fill me with the knowledge of your experiences. I am unlimited so you can create whatever it is you desire. And whatever your choices are, I will always love you because I am the love that gives you everlasting life.

If you choose not to be as I am and you let your body die, then know that you will live on and I will always be with you. You are my beautiful child, the apple of my eye, made from the same substance that I am. I know only to love you for you are what I am. Go forth and explore me and make known what I am'.

As mentioned in the Ramtha quote earlier, Quantum Mechanics is a branch on the tree of the science of God. What you consistently focus upon will eventually become your reality. Only you can undermine your dreams with your doubt. If your 'common thought' remains in the first three seals, then all you're ever going to know and see in your life, is the dimension you're looking at now - quantum

Becoming a Master

fact. But if you shift your consciousness upwards, formulate a new dream, accept that dream as a probability; hold onto that vision with a vice grip until it becomes your common thought: then you've engaged automatic pilot to being your dream. Patience is the vehicle that eventually delivers the dream.

Your environment is addictive, make no mistake about that. It matters not what you are addicted to but that you conquer it! You can be addicted to food, sex, drugs, alcohol, housework, dangerous sports; indeed, anything! As Dr. Joe Dispenza puts it on the brilliant movie 'What the Bleep do we Know?!' "An addiction is simply something you can't stop". So this begs the question, what can't you give up in your life and why? And what are the underlying emotions associated with that? And what flaws in your own psyche are hooking you into those emotions? (refer my article Emotional Mind-Hooks in my other book).

Finally, imagine for a moment what it would have been like for Jesus the Christ. He was hanging there on the cross, battling with the demons of doubt; not entirely sure he could resurrect his body after its death. Nevertheless, he chose to live his truth and he let go of his responsibility for his young daughter and his unborn son in favour of a greater responsibility; namely, the responsibility to himself and to all of mankind. That was his chosen journey to become a Christ. It was him moving his energy from the sixth to the seventh seal. And with his last few breaths he blew away the remnants of this illusionary dimension. (source: Ramtha)

It will be beyond most of us to have such courage in this life to become a Christ (a Master), yet we can still step up the evolutionary ladder by virtue of our own choices. Perhaps our greatest teaching will be our ability to find forgiveness for others and for our own judgements. Individually, this will relieve us of centuries-old 'unfinished business'. In the light of all eternity, is there any one thing that cannot be forgiven and is there any one person who is not worth loving? Don't forgive them and love them for them, do it for yourself! And in doing so you are loving yourself and evolving yourself.

Thank you for buying my book. It has become my soul's map for my future. It has been a pleasure writing this book for myself and for all of my readers. It gives me great pleasure knowing that you are reading one of my books. It has taken me countless hours putting this together but it was worth it and I wouldn't have changed it for the World!

Whatever your desires are in life, I hope my words will help to inspire you in your evolutionary quest. All the very best to you and your family - Gary Bate.

Copyright Gary Bate 2000-2009

Do you know how much Godly power it takes to keep you breathing whilst you're asleep? Miniscule. Imagine if that source of power descended upon you in full force. That's the opportunity of pursuing your own evolution. Of course such power in the wrong hands would be catastrophic - beyond what we could even imagine. That is why this extremely rare occurrence only visits persons who are pure of heart. Authentic power will only come through a pure vessel.

If you have enjoyed this, my book, you will love its sequel, The Question Is ~ Gary Bate.

www.ingramcontent.com/pod-product-compliance
Lightning Source LLC
Chambersburg PA
CBHW072336300426
44109CB00042B/1639